PEER COUNSELING

in Youth Groups

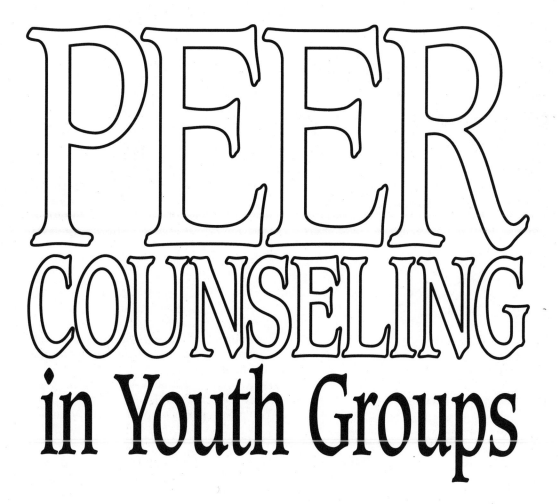

ZONDERVAN/YOUTH SPECIALTIES BOOKS

Professional Resources

Called to Care
Developing Student Leaders
Feeding Your Forgotten Soul
Growing Up in America
High School Ministry
How to Recruit and Train Volunteer Youth Workers
    (Previously released as Unsung Heroes)
Junior High Ministry (Revised Edition)
The Ministry of Nurture
Organizing Your Youth Ministry
Peer Counseling in Youth Groups
The Youth Minister's Survival Guide
Youth Ministry Nuts and Bolts

Discussion Starter Resources

Amazing Tension Getters
Get 'Em Talking
High School TalkSheets
Hot Talks
Junior High TalkSheets
More High School TalkSheets
More Junior High TalkSheets
Option Plays
Parent Ministry TalkSheets
Tension Getters
Tension Getters Two

Special Needs and Issues

The Complete Student Missions Handbook
Divorce Recovery for Teenagers
Ideas for Social Action
Intensive Care: Helping Teenagers in Crisis
Rock Talk
Teaching the Truth About Sex
Up Close and Personal: How to Build Community
    in Your Youth Group

Youth Ministry Programming

Adventure Games
Creative Programming Ideas for Junior High
    Ministry
Creative Socials and Special Events
Good Clean Fun
Good Clean Fun, Volume 2
Great Games for City Kids
Great Ideas for Small Youth Groups
Greatest Skits on Earth
Greatest Skits on Earth, Volume 2
Holiday Ideas for Youth Groups (Revised Edition)

Junior High Game Nights
More Junior High Game Nights
On-Site: 40 On-Location Youth Programs
Play It! Great Games for Groups
Super Sketches for Youth Ministry
Teaching the Bible Creatively
The Youth Specialties Handbook for Great Camps
    and Retreats

4th–6th Grade Ministry

Attention Grabbers for 4th–6th Graders
Great Games for 4th–6th Graders
How to Survive Middle School
Incredible Stories
More Attention Grabbers for 4th–6th Graders
More Great Games for 4th–6th Graders
More Quick and Easy Activities for 4th–6th Graders
Quick and Easy Activities for 4th-6th Graders

Clip Art

ArtSource™ Volume 1—Fantastic Activities
ArtSource™ Volume 2—Borders, Symbols,
    Holidays, and Attention Getters
ArtSource™ Volume 3—Sports
ArtSource™ Volume 4—Phrases and Verses
ArtSource™ Volume 5—Amazing Oddities and
    Appalling Images
ArtSource™ Volume 6—Spiritual Topics
Youth Specialties Clip Art Book
Youth Specialties Clip Art Book, Volume 2

Video

Next Time I Fall In Love Video Curriculum
Understanding Your Teenager Video Curriculum
Video Spots for Junior High Game Nights

Other Books by Joan Sturkie

Acting It Out—with Marsh Cassidy (Resource
    Publications)
Christian Peer Counseling: Love in Action—with
    Gordon Bear (Word)
Enjoy Your Kids: Enjoy Your Work (Word)
Listening with Love (Resource Publications)
The Peer Counselor's Pocket Book—with Valerie
    Gibson (Resource Publications)

Other Books by Siang-Yang Tan

Lay Counseling: Equipping Christians for a Helping
    Ministry (Zondervan)

PEER COUNSELING

in Youth Groups

Equipping your kids to help each other

**Joan Sturkie and
Siang-Yang Tan**

ZondervanPublishingHouse
Grand Rapids, Michigan

A Division of HarperCollinsPublishers

Peer Counseling in Youth Groups

Copyright © 1992 by Youth Specialties, Inc.

Youth Specialties Books, 1224 Greenfield Drive, El Cajon, California 92021, are published by Zondervan Publishing House, 5300 Patterson, SE, Grand Rapids, Michigan 49530

Library of Congress Cataloging-in-Publication Data

Sturkie, Joan, date.
    Peer counseling in youth groups : equipping your kids to help each other / Joan Sturkie, Siang-Yang Tan.
       p. cm.
    Includes bibliographical references.
    ISBN 0-310-54081-X
    1. Church work with teenagers. 2. Peer counseling in the church.
I. Tan, Siang-Yang, date. II. Title.
BV4447.S76 1992
259'.23—dc20   91-17538
                                                                    CIP

Edited by Tim McLaughlin and Kathi George
Cover design by Jack Rogers
Cover photos by Mark Rayburn and Jim Whitmer
Typography by Leah Perry

Printed in the United States of America

93 94 95 96 97 98 99 /   / 10 9 8 7 6 5 4 3 2

To my husband, Roy, and our eight children and two sons-in-law: Alissa and Mike, David, Matthew, Kimberly and Kyle, Paul, Timothy, John, and Elizabeth. And to my grandson, James Trenton Hearon, who will be a teenager in eleven more years and may be a peer counselor in a Christian youth group.

Joan Sturkie

To my wife, Angela; daughter, Carolyn; and son, Andrew: for their love, encouragement, patience, and prayers.

Siang-Yang Tan

Contents

Since the laws on liability, confidentiality, and mandatory reporting may vary from state to state, when in doubt, have your forms and peer counseling guidelines reviewed by qualified legal counsel.

Foreword

A few days after I finished reading the manuscript for this book, I met with a group of church leaders (mostly pastors) for a brainstorming session about their counseling ministries. Most of these people have seminary training, and one even has a doctorate in counseling. But they presented a similar message.

"We never learned how to help people," they said. "We read books and learned about counseling theory, but our professors failed to prepare us for the problems that are brought to our offices almost every day. We don't know how to keep from getting burned out, when to make a referral, how to help people who don't have insurance or money for professional counseling, or how to prevent problems in the first place."

Soon we were into a conversation that Joan Sturkie and Siang-Yang Tan would have liked. The church leaders in our little group concluded that Christians must find ways to help one another, like the Scriptures command (Gal. 6:2, 10). "We need support groups," someone argued. "Churches need to work together to help meet the needs of hurting people," said another. More than one talked about the need to find practical ways (not fancy psychological theories) to equip lay people to minister to each other's needs.

This book provides those kinds of equipping tools. It is a user-friendly, highly practical book about helping kids.

Recently the Search Institute in Minneapolis studied 33,000 young people in grades nine to twelve. The group was divided into two: those who spent time every week volunteering to help others, including "people who are poor, hungry, sick, or unable to care for themselves," and those who never participated in such activities. When the groups were compared, the people helpers were found to have more caring values, greater participation in churches or synagogues, more involvement in youth organizations like Scouts or 4-H, better self-esteem, and stronger relationship and social skills. According to the researchers, the best way to stimulate caring in young people is to have adult models who are both exemplary caregivers and who encourage caring in teenagers.

This book is designed to help you develop that kind of caring behavior in kids. The authors give useful, relevant, biblically based guidelines for "equipping your kids to help each other." There is no attempt to force all of us into some rigid training model. Instead, each reader can tailor the following instructional materials to fit the available training times, the personalities of both the instructor and the trainees, and each young counselor's level of maturity. For some, this program will be a first step, leading to more advanced counselor training. For most, it will be a core introduction to effective people-helping skills. For others, this could be a one-shot course that will help them relate to others more effectively as they go through life, even if they never get involved in lay counseling activities.

Authors Sturkie and Tan have given us a tool that many church leaders will find helpful. Their book is a model of the kind of resource that those pastors in the brainstorming group are seeking. I suspect that many others, especially youth leaders, will turn often to the following pages as they look for guidance in teaching and establishing effective peer counseling programs.

Gary R. Collins, Ph.D.

Introduction

It was a typically bland high school cafeteria, but tonight it was filled with colorful balloons and streamers. What surprised me was the number of people in the room. A year earlier I had attended a similar banquet at this school with less than a quarter of tonight's guests.

Amid the happy chaos of celebration, 250 parents, teachers, students, and friends had come to see sixty-seven high school students become official peer counselors on campus. The graduation ceremony signified that these young people had successfully completed a semester's work in peer counseling training and were now qualified to support and help their peers. With the diverse and critical problems teenagers encounter in today's world, these teens would make a difference on this campus. In fact, the small banner hanging on the podium summed it up: "Who You Are Makes a Difference."

As I sat and watched these young people go across the stage and receive their certificates (and shirts with "Peers Helping Peers" printed across the backs), loud applause arose from one corner of the room. Sitting together in a group were last year's eighteen peer counseling graduates, here to support this new group. They had all come a long way in the two years since I had been called to this school as a peer counseling consultant to assist in starting a program.

That night in the cafeteria I felt a longing to see such a night repeated in a church or parachurch setting. What if this was happening with sixty-seven *Christian* young people, I thought, who were being trained and commissioned to go out and help their peers, serving under the banner of Jesus Christ? Isn't that what we are all supposed to do as Christians, anyway—"carry each other's burdens," as Galatians 6:2 puts it?

Young people trained in school settings are now spearheading peer counseling programs in their church youth groups. (Some of the school groups are called "peer helping" groups or "peer listening" groups or "TLC: Teens Listening and Caring," but it's all the same thing.) We need to support these teens. They know the pain and hurt many of their peers are feeling because they are with them every day—at school, on the telephone, in the malls, at games. These young people want to be prepared to reach out and help their friends.

We have written this book to promote the concept of peer counseling and to help youth leaders establish programs in their churches and parachurch organizations. Joan Sturkie is the primary writer, so the first-person references are to her. Formerly a high school counselor and a peer counseling teacher, she is now a trainer and consultant. Sturkie is the mother of eight children. Siang-Yang Tan, Ph.D., has provided this book with its biblical perspectives and has contributed significantly to its writing. A former Youth for Christ leader and youth director, he now is associate professor of psychology and director of the doctor of psychology program at Fuller Seminary's Graduate School of Psychology. He is the father of two children.

Young people and their needs are very close to the hearts of both authors. How do we reach those young people and assist them with their needs? The answer is by teaching them to help each other. And peer counseling has proven to be very effective at this. By being trained as peer counselors, young people learn how to reach out and help their peers in need.

The skills that kids in your youth group will acquire will be available to them throughout their lives. Active listening, for instance, immediately opens the door for better communications with parents, teachers, employers, and friends.

Peer Counseling in Youth Groups explains what peer counseling is, how it works, and exactly what it can do for your youth group. Many youth leaders are already aware of their teenagers' enormous potential for helping each other. Teens are just waiting for a qualified adult to teach them to use the talents God has given them. Young people are known for their bountiful energy, their desire for social interactions—and their ability to talk long hours on the telephone. Why not put all of these assets to good use?

Besides learning how to help each other, young people find that something very special happens in the peer counseling group. After only a few weeks, you'll begin hearing "I like being here because this feels like a family," and "I feel like I belong. I've never felt like I've fit into a group before, but for the first time I feel I can be my true self and be accepted. I can just be me."

Peer counseling is a great way to bond members of your youth group together and make everyone feel accepted. Even if no one ever helps anyone outside the group, the tremendous good that has been accomplished within the peer counseling class will be reward enough for setting up the program.

Do not fear, however, that the trainees will become complacent and not want to help others. It works in reverse. As they learn to help each other in the group, they recognize the skills they now have and are eager to put them to use outside their own circle.

Public schools and organizations are already using peer counseling extensively. Peer counseling has expanded because it is effective.[1] It is time for Christians to train our own. What better place to start than with our youth groups?

In order to protect the confidentiality of counselees and others, case studies and examples used in this book are based on composites of real-life situations.

Joan Sturkie
Siang-Yang Tan

SECTION ONE:

Peer Counseling and Your Ministry

WHY PEER COUNSELING?

What's the matter with my kid?" parents asked me when I was a high school counselor. "What's wrong with teenagers today?"

One such parent was in my office, trying to understand her son. Tom was truant frequently and was failing many of his subjects. "I wish I understood what is going on with Tom," she said, shaking her head. "His dad and I have worked hard to give him everything he needs—nice clothes, spending money—and he works just ten hours a week at a part-time job. But all he wants to do is hang out with a bunch of kids who play that awful music. He's letting a good education go right down the tube. I just don't understand teenagers . . . why are they like this today?"

What exactly *are* teenagers like today? What are their problems?

• Despite a drop in cocaine use among most high schoolers, more than half of them still drink, and as many as a third have indulged in binge drinking (five or more drinks at a time).[1] More than a third use tobacco.[2]

• Half of America's teens are sexually active. Forty percent of teen pregnancies end in abortion. These account for a quarter of all U.S. abortions. The number of teen AIDS cases is small, but it's doubling every fourteen months—and they're getting it primarily heterosexually.[3]

• An estimated 600,000 teenage girls and 300,000 teenage boys work as prostitutes. Their average age is fifteen.[4]

• Although only 8 percent say they tried suicide, a quarter of teens say they "thought seriously" about killing themselves.[5]

• No more than a quarter of U.S. teens are overweight, but nearly half of high school females are trying to lose weight. Of those who perceive themselves overweight, nearly a quarter have tried vomiting.[6]

• Adolescents are responsible for nearly 40 percent of all serious crimes (murder, rape, larceny).[7] Eighty percent of deaths in the fifteen-to-twenty-four age group are secondary to accidents, suicides, and homicides.[8]

In 1989, the Carnegie Council on Adolescent Development presented the following information in *Turning Points: Preparing American Youth for the 21st Century:*[9]

• One in four adolescents is subject to high-risk behaviors and school failure.

• Fifty-six percent of students in the graduating class of 1987 began drinking in their sixth- to ninth-grade years.

• One-fourth of all sexually active adolescents will become infected with a sexually transmitted disease before graduating from high school.

• Forty-four percent of black males, 33 percent of black females, 30 percent of white males, and 22 percent of white females are one or more years below expected grade level.

• A recent National Assessment of Educational Progress (NAEP) found that only 11 percent of thirteen-year-olds were "adept" readers.[10]

• Each year's class of dropouts will, over a lifetime, cost the nation about $260 billion in lost earnings and foregone taxes.

• Of teens who give birth, 46 percent will go on welfare within four years; of unmarried teens who give birth, 73 percent will be on welfare within four years.

Is the church helping these teenagers? Unfortunately, teenagers are the least-churched age group we have: 80 to 85 percent of teenagers are not significantly involved in the church.

Yet we believe the Christian church *can* help these young people by establishing Christian peer counseling programs in youth groups and teaching young people how to care for each other.

What exactly is peer counseling?

How is it used? How specifically can it be used with Christian young people?

Peer counseling can be defined in several different ways. In peer counseling, adolescents learn how to appropriately and positively support one another. It is empathic, paraprofessional communication that involves knowledge and skills often used by professional therapists.

Peer counseling is "the use of active listening and problem-solving skills," write Vincent D' Andrea and Peter Salovey in *Peer Counseling: Skills and Perspectives*, "along with knowledge about human growth and mental health, to counsel people who are our peers—peers in age, status, and knowledge."[11]

Peer counseling is a mode of interpersonal sharing in which a trained person provides help and support to one or more individuals.

What is a peer counselor, then?

"A peer counselor is a person who cares about others and takes time to listen to their problems," explained a girl in one of my classes. "By using active listening and other counseling skills, we help counselees clarify their feelings and look for available solutions."

Peers helping peers is not a new concept. Children have been taught and encouraged to function as instructional agents for their classroom peers since the early 1800s. It was not until the late 1960s, however, that peer counseling was rigorously studied. It has been used since then with increasing acceptance and success. With student problems being spotlighted during the 1980s and increasing demands on high school counselors' time, peer counseling has spread to schools throughout the country. It is now found in elementary, middle, and high schools across the United States and in some foreign countries.

State peer counseling organizations have been formed, and some annual conferences record an attendance of 4,000 or more. A National Peer Helpers Association attracts people from all fifty states to its annual conference. State organizations and a national organization publish newsletters that allow the membership to network with each other.

Although schools may be the largest users of peer counseling, they are not the only ones benefitting from the program. Businesses, halfway houses, law enforcement agencies, social agencies, senior citizen centers, and churches also use peer counseling.

What then is *Christian* peer counseling?

Christian peer counseling is support and assistance given by a Christian, in service to Jesus Christ, to another person in need who is a peer in age, status, or knowledge. The primary focus is on truthful and empathic communication, with appropriate use of spiritual resources such as prayer and the Bible. The Christian peer counselor should be trained in all helping skills and techniques that are consistent with the values and virtues of Christlike living. He or she relies on the Holy Spirit for divine wisdom, power, and love.

To follow Christ's commandment to "carry each other's burdens" (Gal. 6:2), young people in our churches must be trained. Since we already know that the needs of young people present a field that is white unto harvest and that the laborers (that's you) are few—and since both common sense and statistical evidence show that peers listen to each other—then the logical conclusion is that peer counseling needs to be established in our churches and parachurch organizations. A few churches are already successfully doing this. Yet if schools and social agencies are helping young people with such programs, isn't it the responsibility of the church to step to the forefront and take its rightful place at the head of the movement to teach young people to love one another and to reach out in Christian service to their peers? You may be the one in your church to help your young people by establishing this program.

Know at least this about peer counseling . . .

- *A need exists.* Hardly a day goes by that the media do not proclaim the dire straits our young people are in. They do this in their stories of teenage suicide, school dropouts, pregnancy and abortion, runaways, drug and alcohol addiction, eating disorders, and family discord. Christian people do not have to read or hear the stories in the media to know that a need exists. They have only to look in their own or a friend's home.

• *Peer counseling fills that need.* Peer counseling is no longer the new kid on the block. A proven concept, it has been tested in public and private schools across the nation and has proved to be an effective tool in helping young people. Many schools who waited to see how it worked in other educational institutions similar to theirs now are convinced of its value and have started programs of their own. In 1991, 4,000 students and their teachers attended the seventh annual California Peer Counseling Association conference to proclaim their belief in this program. State conferences similar to this one are conducted in other areas of the United States. Probably some young people in your Christian youth group belong to a peer counseling class in their school, and they will be a great help to you in getting a program started in your church or organization. Peers truly are an important resource in meeting the needs of today's youths, and it is time that churches and Christian organizations take their rightful place in training and mobilizing these young people for Christian service in their own community.

• *Peer counseling is biblically sound.* When Jesus carried out his earthly ministry, he walked among the people and listened to the accounts of their everyday living problems. He instructs us to do likewise. In the parable of the Good Samaritan (Luke 10:25–37), Jesus asks, "Which of these three do you think was a neighbor to the man who fell into the hands of robbers?" The answer comes in verse 37: "The expert in the law replied, 'The one who had mercy on him.' Jesus told him, 'Go and do likewise.'" In Galatians 6:2 we read, "Carry each other's burdens, and in this way you will fulfill the law of Christ." Then in John 15:12, Jesus' words come across clearly: "My command is this: Love each other as I have loved you." We can follow this command only if we reach out to others. Peer counseling is a tool we use in learning how to extend arms.

• *Peer counseling is affordable.* One of the reasons peer counseling has been so effective in churches is because it does not cost a lot of money. The training of the youth leader (by attending a workshop or by having a peer counseling consultant come on site) and the purchasing of books are the main expenses involved in getting a program started. Once the program is underway, the expenses of running it are minimal. The beauty of peer counseling is that the peer counselors donate their time, thus eliminating a fee to be paid for all the counseling hours provided. Peer counseling is a program that can work for any size church or organization.

THE BIBLE AND PEER COUNSELING

Ayouth minister was stopped by a parent in the church hall one Sunday morning. "What's this peer counseling stuff really all about?" the parent asked. "Isn't it just secular counseling based on worldly values that actually can undermine Christian principles? What does the Bible say about peer counseling?"

Church leaders, high school staff members, and even students often ask these questions when they are first exposed to the idea of Christian peer counseling. Initiating a peer counseling ministry because young people value friendship and have many needs and struggles is a good reason to *start* a peer counseling program, but it is not enough. There needs to be more. You can find a sound biblical basis for a peer counseling ministry in passages like Luke 10:25–37, Galatians 6:2, John 15:12, and 1 Thessalonians 5:14.

Beyond a biblical foundation, however, there is also a distinctly biblical perspective from which to counsel, so that Christian values and principles will not be contradicted or undermined by secular philosophy or worldly values.

WHAT HUMAN NATURE IS ALL ABOUT

Christian peer counselors need a clearly biblical view of human nature or humanity. This view includes the following:[1]

• *Basic psychological and spiritual needs* of human beings include security (love), significance (meaning/impact), and hope (forgiveness), all of which underlie a fundamental need for an adequate sense of self-worth or self-acceptance (to be distinguished from selfishness or self-centeredness). Such needs are ultimately met only in the context of a personal relationship with Jesus Christ as one's Lord and Savior. Trying desperately to meet such needs apart from Christ, however, fallen human beings pursue personal achievements, pleasure, personal relationships, prestige, power, physical beauty, or strength—but these do not last and cannot fulfill individuals' basic needs in a deeper way.

• *The basic problem of human beings has to do with sin.* The breaking of God's moral standards as revealed in the Bible and the satanic belief that we can handle our own concerns and fulfill our basic needs or longings apart from God are at the root of most mental/emotional problems that do not have obvious organic bases or biological causes. Not all emotional suffering is due to personal sin, however, or even the sins of others. Emotional and spiritual anguish or suffering sometimes may be part of God's process of helping his children grow to become more like Jesus. Even Jesus himself suffered anguish or deep distress in the Garden of Gethsemane when he struggled with his Father's will of going to the cross to die for a sinful world (Matt. 26:36–39; Mark 14:32–36; Luke 22:40–44)—but he never sinned (Heb. 4:15). He obeyed his Father's will. We need to distinguish sin-induced mental/emotional suffering from anguish or deep distress that may be part of growing as a Christian in obedience to God's will.

• *The ultimate goal of human beings* is to know and enjoy God—that is, to nurture and enjoy spiritual health. Therefore the ultimate goal of Christian counseling, including Christian peer counseling, is holiness or Christlikeness (Rom. 8:29), and not temporal happiness. In other words, it is spiritual health and not just mental/emotional or physical health.

• *Problem feelings,* like crippling anxiety or fear and severe depression, are usually, but not always, due to problem behavior and, more fundamentally, problem thinking (see John 8:32; Rom. 12:1–2; Eph. 4:22–24; and Phil. 4:8). For example, it's easy for a teenager to feel down because she had a bad grade on a test. "I really bombed this time," she thinks. "It's terrible to get a C on this test. I'll never be able to face my teachers again—and my parents will be upset, too. My whole world is caving in . . . I can't take this failure!" Extremely negative thinking like this leads to bad feelings, including depression. Another kid who thinks more reasonably and less negatively ("I'm disappointed with a C, but it's not the end of the world. I'll do better next time.") may feel saddened and disappointed, but not depressed.

Problem thinking is not the root of all emotional problems, however. Biological factors, such as chemical imbalances in the brain's functioning, may underlie some types of problem feelings. In cases of manic-depressive disorder, for instance, with its extreme mood swings between elation and depression, medications may be needed and psychiatric or medical consultation should be sought.

Don't discount the possiblity of demonic forces, either. Some severe emotional problems may be due to demonization—or demonic oppression or even possession. Use discernment in such cases. If the demonic is clearly at work, you'll probably need fasting, praying for deliverance, and exorcism. If you suspect demonic complications in your counseling, consult pastors and other church leaders experienced in ministry to the demonized.

• *A holistic view of persons*—that is, a view that acknowledges physical, mental/emotional, social, and spiritual dimensions of human functioning—is essential. Jesus himself grew in all these areas, reports Luke 2:52—in wisdom (mental/emotional), stature (physical), and in favor with God (spiritual) and men (social). Human problems should therefore be viewed in the context of all four of these areas of life. The emotional problems of a genuinely fatigued and depressed high schooler may be due simply to insufficient and irregular sleep—all because he's been cramming several days for final exams.

BIBLICAL DISTINCTIVES OF PEER COUNSELING[2]

• *The Holy Spirit's ministry as counselor is crucial* (John 14:16,

17). Depend on him in prayer and yield to his control and guidance, especially during the peer counseling session, asking for his wisdom and love as well as his healing power to flow through you to touch and help the counselee.

• *The Bible is a basic and comprehensive guide* (though not an exhaustive one) to human functioning and dysfunctioning, and therefore a guide also for peer counseling or helping people with their problems (see 2 Tim. 3:16, 17). Counselors must know what the Bible says about particular issues, problems, or struggles.[3] When appropriate, counselors should use the Scriptures to provide guidance and instruction in specific areas, especially when helping other Christian peers. Being nonjudgmental does not mean that counselors do not have values or directions from the Bible, but rather that counselors do not condemn others even if they have sinned or done wrong. Further, it means that we still love and accept sinners as people of worth who are precious to the Lord. Guidance and even loving confrontation based on biblical values and teaching, however, may be necessary at times—nor is this inconsistent with being nonjudgmental, if it is done in a spirit of love and compassion.

• *Prayer is an integral or essential part of biblical counseling* (James 5:16). Counselors must pray for the peers they counsel, asking for the Holy Spirit's wisdom and healing power to work in and through them, so that they may be significantly touched and made more whole by the Lord's healing grace. Counselors should pray for counselees regularly—before, during, and after the counseling session. If the counselee does not want to be prayed for aloud, the counselor can still pray silently during the session. Praying with the counselee, whether aloud or silently, is appropriate and helpful if the counselee desires it. James 5:16 instructs us to confess our faults or sins to one another and to pray for one another that we may be healed.

• *The ultimate goal of counseling is maturity in Christ* for counselees who are already Christians (Romans 8:29) and the fulfillment of the Great Commission for counselees who are not yet Christians (Matt. 28:18–20). Witnessing to non-Christian counselees can be an important part of Christian peer counseling, but it must be done lovingly, sensitively, and gently. Teenagers with personal problems don't need the gospel of Jesus Christ shoved down their throats. Yet at the right time it can be shared in a caring way with non-Christian counselees who are seeking for and open to a new, personal relationship with Jesus Christ as their own Lord and Savior.

• *The personal spiritual qualities of the peer counselor should include:* goodness or love, knowledge of the Bible (Rom. 15:14), wisdom (Col. 3:16), maturity (Gal. 6:1, 2) and the spiritual gift of exhortation or encouragement (Rom. 12:8).

• *The counselee's attitudes, motivations, and desire for help are also important.* Research shows that counselees who are not hostile or mistrustful and who are actively involved in their counseling do better than those who are withdrawn or defensive.

• *The relationship between the peer counselor and the counselee is another significant factor in effective peer counseling.* The ingredients for rapport and communication include *empathy* (understanding), *respect or warmth* (caring for the counselee), *concreteness* (being specific), *genuineness* (being real), *confrontation* (telling it like it is), and *immediacy* (what's really going on between the two of you). Speaking the truth in love is how the Bible describes it (Eph. 4:15).

• *Peer counseling involves exploration, understanding, and action phases, with a focus on changing problem thinking.* A Christian peer counselor must *explore* and try to *understand* the counselee and his or her problems as well as possible before moving on to the *action* phase: active problem solving and appropriate advice giving. This requires the Christian peer counselor, first and foremost, to *listen actively* to the counselee.

• *Peer counseling is flexible* (1 Thess. 5:14). Jesus' style of relating or helping was flexible. He possessed a prophetic, confrontational style (with Nicodemus in John 3, for instance), a priestly, accepting style (with the woman caught in adultery in John 8), and a pastoral style (with the Samaritan woman in John 4).

• *The specific techniques or methods of counseling used should be consistent with Scripture or biblical teaching and values* (1 Thess. 5:21). Cognitive behavioral methods, including problem solving and role-playing (to learn particular social skills or coping techniques), may be especially helpful—but they have their limitations.

• *Peer counselors need cultural sensitivity and cross-cultural counseling skills* (Chapter Seven explains how cultural diversity affects peer counseling).

• *Skills in outreach and prevention are also important.* Peer counselors need training in realizing how environmental stresses like poverty, unemployment, racism, sexism, and lack of social support can lead to emotional problems. Peer counselors also need to learn how to help counselees connect with appropriate sources of community help and social support, including church and parachurch youth groups.

• *Peer counselors must recognize their own limitations and must learn referral skills.* Counselors should seek supervision and guidance from more mature Christian counselors or leaders (especially from the peer counseling director or leader)—but remember not to break confidentiality guidelines. Peer counselors should refer counselees to more experienced or professional counselors, including pastors or other church leaders, when necessary or appropriate.

"SENIORITIS"—A CASE STUDY

In his senior year of high school, Mike was floundering, confused and indecisive about his future. Should he go to college? What should he major in? Or should he start working at a full-time job? What type of job? These questions troubled him enough that he decided to speak to Fernando, a Christian peer counselor in his church youth group.

Fernando listened patiently and prayerfully as Mike poured out his frustrations and fears. He helped Mike explore a wider range of options, including part-time work and enrollment in a community college.

It became apparent as the peer counseling proceeded that Mike wanted clearer guidance from God regarding his future. He realized with Fernando's help that he needed a closer relationship with God in order to discern his will. During the peer counseling sessions, Fernando often prayed with Mike. With this spiritual support, Mike developed a more regular devotional time in prayer and Bible reading each day. With these came more peace and more intimacy with God.

He eventually felt that God wanted him to use his life to help others. He enrolled in college as a psychology major with the intent of becoming a professional counselor. While in college he worked part-time as an assistant youth minister at a large urban church. Mike will always be grateful for the help he received from Fernando, who provided peer counseling from a biblical perspective.

Mike and Fernando's peer counseling relationship is a good example of how God can use the peer counseling process, applied within a biblical framework, to help kids work through difficult situations and make tough decisions in a healthy, spiritually nurturing fashion.

SECTION TWO:

Starting a Peer Counseling Program

LAYING THE GROUNDWORK

P at was never one to let any grass grow under her feet. The day after she returned from a peer counseling conference, she briefly mentioned to her senior pastor her desire to start a peer counseling ministry in the youth group. Bruce seemed pleased enough with the idea. The following Sunday she poured her enthusiasm into the young people and immediately asked for volunteers to be trained as peer counselors. Many responded. It was working—just as the conference speaker had predicted!

That is, until one day when Pat was called into Bruce's office. After a lengthy discussion about her program, Pat found Bruce to be less enthusiastic than he had appeared at their brief initial meeting. Bruce had apparently been questioned by some church board members who had kids in the month-old peer counseling training program. Although the parents did not have any specific complaints about the program, they wondered why they had not been informed about what they assumed was a new direction the youth ministry was taking. Was peer counseling to replace the group's evangelistic emphasis the board had approved for the following year? Would there be money available to support this new program?

Pat soon realized that she had implemented the peer counseling program too hastily. Though the program was as good as the conference speaker had said it was, in her enthusiam Pat had neglected to lay down sufficient groundwork. Pat suspended the training program until she could obtain the full support of Bruce and the church board. A full year passed before she realized her dream of starting a peer counseling program.

Pat learned the hard way what she needed to do before she ever asked for teenage volunteer counselors. To avoid a similar mistake, you will want to follow the preparatory steps listed below before starting a peer counseling program.

Pray

Like any other step in our Christian lives, the decision to start a peer counseling program requires much prayer. Seeking God's will in his time frame is crucial. In Philippians 4:6 we are told, "Do not be anxious about anything, but in everything, by prayer and petition, with thanksgiving, present your requests to God." After asking for God's will and seeking his guidance, wait for his answer. God speaks to different people in different ways, and your sustained desire to see this program started may indicate God's approval of the project.

Seek support for the program from key church leaders

If you feel that it is God's will (and given with his blessing) that a peer counseling program be started in your group, then the next step is to gain the support of others in the church or organization.

Most of us resist change to some degree, and this is particularly true if it involves a new concept or idea that is unfamiliar to us. Because *peer counseling* is not a common phrase, you'll need to solicit key people in your church or organization to help sell the idea. Usually the desire to start a program originates with only one person—an individual who took in a peer counseling workshop at a conference, or someone who may have come in contact with a relative or friend who received training. This person must then get other leaders interested if a program is to get off the ground.

The place to start is probably with the youth director. (If the individual originally interested in peer counseling *is* the youth director, so much the better. For the purposes of this chapter, let's assume that you, the youth director, are that person.) Next, talk to your immediate supervisor—typically the senior pastor.

After first providing him or her with available literature on the subject and time to look it over, make an appointment to sit down and answer questions the pastor may have. To this meeting invite someone who is familiar with peer counseling and knows how effective it is, and who also has the respect and the ear of the pastor.

Before you can begin an effective, ongoing peer counseling program, you must have the total support of the leadership. This is not to say that everyone must be as excited as you about the program, nor convinced that it is as effective as you say it is—but they must be committed to supporting it as they would support any other program of your church or organization.

The program is not as an island, but rather another finger on the hand of existing programs. It stands separately and distinctly with its own identity, yet at the same time is a part of the whole ministry of your church or organization. If you want the program to be accepted by members of the pastoral staff not directly related to the program, familiarize them with peer counseling, and gain their support. Informal lunches or dinners are often prime settings for such conversations—but however you do it, explain the program and listen to the feelings and questions of the staff. Make sure they especially understand two things clearly:

- *The term "peer counseling."* Definitions have been given earlier in this book, but church leaders may not want a formal definition. "Just tell me what you are talking about," they may say. An easy way to answer their request is to tell them that peer counseling is an effective way to help kids reach out to their friends and help them with their everyday problems. Sure, Christians are supposed to be doing that anyway, but they sometimes hesitate because they feel inadequate and fear doing or saying the wrong thing. With training, teenagers can acquire skills in communication and self-awareness, and these skills will help even the most timid souls to gain confidence and become more effective in their outreach.

- *The mission of the program.* To support a program, Christians need to know that a need exists, that this particular program will fill that need, that it is biblically sound, and that it is affordable. Make sure you cover these points well (see Chapter One for details).

Know the bumps in the road before you start your program

If you know about them ahead of time, you can avoid some of them altogether. Do not become discouraged, however, for some are virtually unavoidable. Just keep working and know that the benefits of peer counseling far exceed the difficulties that come along.

• *Some will criticize the program.* Because peer counseling is relatively new in our churches and parachurch organizations, few people understand what it is or what it does. History tells us that if people do not understand a new idea, they will often take potshots at it out of ignorance or simply because they do not like change. The senior pastor of a local church for twenty-five years was pressured to start a peer counseling program. He initially resisted because he felt peer counseling would take too much time, energy, and too many resources away from his church's number-one priority, evangelism. He often talked disparagingly about peer counseling, not realizing it was actually another tool for evangelistic outreach. The pastor eventually changed his mind after a clergy friend in town told him how many new young people had started attending his church as a result of a peer counseling ministry.

• *Some will feel threatened by the program.* By seeing the excitement a strong peer counseling program creates, they may feel their favorite project is being diminished. This was true of Sam, a Sunday school teacher with a small class of poor attenders. John, on the other hand, taught the peer counselors each week in a well-attended meeting. When Sam realized that several of the kids enrolled in both his and John's classes were faithful attenders at John's class rather than his, he unfortunately saw this as a personal indictment of his teaching and leadership abilities and was consequently unenthusiastic about the peer counseling program. If people see peer counseling as a competitor, they will not support it.

• *Some people simply do not believe in empowering young people.* There are always a few adults in any group who feel very negative about teenagers anyway, and the idea of allowing young people to help each other goes against their mind-set. Young people should be told what to do by adults because, after all, the adults have the wisdom and experience to make right choices. Those who hold this opinion may be well-meaning, good Christian people, but they are insecure, afraid to relinquish control to allow young people to develop their own decision-making skills.

Other individuals may have similar feelings about this subject, but without negative feelings about teenagers. They are the adults who want to work with young people because they thoroughly enjoy them *and* because they enjoy the feeling of power it gives to them. These individuals do not empower youths because it means giving up some of their own power. I encountered teachers like this when I taught peer counseling in the school system, and I know how detrimental such people can be to a program—especially if they volunteer to be actively involved in the training program. What makes it difficult is that these are good people—but they do not make good peer counseling leaders. I have seen mature peer counseling programs almost destroyed when the leader moved away and the person appointed to fill the vacancy was a qualified, good, but controlling person who did not want to empower the young people.

• *If church leadership changes, your program may come under scrutiny and may even lose some of its support.* In the third year of a very successful high school peer counseling program, both the principal and the district superintendent resigned. I was shocked when their replacements did not give me and the program the same previously felt support. I never dreamed the new leadership would not be thoroughly supportive. After all, the program was effective for the students, respected by the parents, a model to other schools. However, they had their own agenda, their own pet projects they wanted to push. This may also be true of a church or parachurch organization if the leadership changes. If you continue to work your program—even if you don't feel total support—you may gain that support in the months to come.

• *Your physical and emotional energy may plummet to low points at times.* We know how exhausting it is to work with young people. Keeping up with their enormous energy can keep some of us hopping. Yet when the physical body becomes weary, you need to rest, to call in your backup person—someone who knows your program well and will follow your instructions. Just a brief rest may give you the extra energy you need.

And there will be times when things are just not going well in the training sessions. A teenage counselor may have broken confidentiality, for instance. This is never supposed to happen, of course, but in reality it does happen once in a while. Gayle was fourteen, the daughter of divorced parents and a peer counselor in training. During one of the training sessions, she confided to the other peer counselors—including her friend Pete—that she would soon be moving to San Francisco to live with her father. Later that week, in a conversation between Pete and Brad, Gayle's sixteen-year-old brother, Brad mentioned that a change was soon to happen in his family. Assuming that Brad was referring to Gayle's forthcoming move, Pete asked how he felt about his sister leaving. Brad knew nothing of Gayle's decision, and Pete realized that he had unintentionally broken confidentiality. He reported this to the class the next week. Pete's candid confession at the next training class devastated everyone, but after a couple of weeks the group managed to get back to its previous trusting stage.

When something like this happens, your emotional energy may dwindle when you realize you must go backward and bond the group again instead of going forward to new skill development. But if you look at these times as just another predictable bump in the road, it will be easier for you to stay focused on the big picture of training the young people to become the best peer counselors in town.

GETTING STARTED: THE NUTS AND BOLTS

I t had been a while since Joel had felt this energized. His car couldn't get him back to his church office fast enough. Joel had just spent a long lunch with a high school teacher who directed a school peer counseling program. The teacher had no end of success stories about his students. My youth group needs this, Joel thought.

At church that afternoon he met one of his adult volunteers in the hall. "How'd your appointment go?" he asked Joel. "Glad you asked," Joel said, and then launched into a recitation of the glories of a peer counseling program for the youth group.

Then the volunteer began asking questions. What rooms and equipment would be needed? What would it cost? Who would direct the program? How would the peer counselor trainees be chosen? When would classes be scheduled? How would confidentiality be maintained? How did peer counseling fit into the total program of the church?

At this point Joel realized that he needed specific answers to these questions if he were ever to see a peer counseling program in his group.

This chapter will help you formulate your own answers to questions like these—before you're put on the spot by a boss, a staffer, or a parent.

The logistics of a peer counseling program are as critical as its philosophy.

STEPS TO BEGIN THE PROGRAM . . .

1. Get a facility.

The training room should be large enough to accommodate twenty to twenty-five people. The educational experience will probably be more productive if the surroundings are conducive to learning. This means a well-lighted room with comfortable chairs (more about this later).

On the other hand, don't shelve peer counseling simply because you don't have ideal rooms. A public school teacher was forced to convert an empty book-storage room into a training facility. Too small for chairs, she decided—so she got a big area rug for the room, and all twenty of the trainees sat in a circle on the floor during the training sessions. It was one of the best peer counseling classes I've ever observed.

For the one-on-one counseling sessions that begin after peer counselors are trained, a small room or office should be made available. Although many of the counseling pairs will meet away from church, most counselees will probably call the church office to make an appointment, and so the initial meetings will likely occur on the premises.

Some programs devote a room to walk-in appointments only and rotate teenage counselors so there's always one on site after school every afternoon.

Don't worry if you must share another department's Sunday school rooms. Chances are, they're used only one or two hours a week anyway, so they're probably available during the rest of the week. After all, if peer counselors are anything, they're flexible. What you do need of your own, however, is a storage place for materials and a file cabinet that can be locked for the confidential records.

2. Develop a budget.

Although starting a program is relatively inexpensive, it warrants a line of its own in the church or organization's budget. Expenses are minimal, but a program needs funding for materials and a director's salary—unless, of course, the director is already on staff and salaried as a youth pastor. The job description must be tailored to encompass the supervision of a peer counseling program. Alternatively, a director could be a volunteer and therefore require no salary at all. In some adult church peer counseling programs, a donation envelope is provided for the counselees to contribute for the services they have received. In youth groups, however, a donation is not normally requested, nor do we recommend such a practice. (See a sample "Budget Worksheet" on p. 44.)

3. Recruit a director.

Whether this person is a staff or lay person, he or she should be someone who relates well to young people, believes in the program, and has the time to commit to the project (typically, about ten hours a week). Since this is also an administrative job, the person will need skills in supervision, record keeping, and implementation of policies and procedures. (See "Job Description: Director of Peer Counseling," on p. 45.)

4. Recruit a supervisor.

In a small church or organization the director of peer counseling may do everything. In larger ones, however, he or she may delegate most of the everyday operations of the program to the supervisor. The director may choose someone who has had training as a mental health professional (a psychologist, family counselor, social worker, school counselor, or psychiatric nurse) and who, in fact, may be better qualified than the director to handle the supervision of the advanced counselors. Supervisor is a volunteer, part-time position that is often rotated on a yearly basis. More than one supervisor may be needed in larger churches. Typically, a supervisor will be involved about five hours a week.

5. Select trainees.

This aspect of peer counseling needs a fuller discussion than there is room for here. See Chapter Five, "Selecting Your Peer Counselor Trainees."

6. Schedule classes.

You'll need to invest a minimum of forty-five to sixty hours of training in your students before they are qualified to counsel their peers.

Some groups meet two hours a week in the evening; others on Saturday mornings for four hours; others start the training with a weekend retreat—eight hours a day for two days—then complete the hours on a weekly basis. The way your sessions are scheduled and the number of sessions you will need to cover each unit will depend on your needs and time commitments. You determine class times, with sensitivity to your teenagers' personal schedules.

In short, design a schedule that works for your group—then adhere to it so all trainees may plan their time accordingly.

The schedule of sessions for the entire training should be completed *before* the first class begins. Distribute copies of the schedule to the trainees at the first class meeting. A brief discussion and question period will give the trainees an opportunity to clarify any misunderstandings of dates or times.

7. Prepare your forms.

Be prepared *before* the first class begins. This includes having enough of the appropriate forms ready to distribute to your trainees. The most important of these forms are the **application form** (see Chapter Five, p. 54); the **confidentiality contract** (see Chapter Five, p. 56); and the **parent consent letter** (see Chapter Five, p. 55). We have supplied a sample confidentiality contract. You may choose to write your own or reproduce this one and distribute copies to your trainees. They should sign them and turn them in during the first training session.

8. Gather your curriculum materials for the training classes.

For instance, make copies of the hand-out sheets for students that appear in Units 1 through 10 of this book. Do this six weeks before the first class begins. Having things in place the first time the young people walk through the door will give everyone the feeling that peer counseling is a well-thought-out program.

9. Make your meeting room appealing and comfortable.

Pay attention to the thermostat—walking into a cold room in the winter or a hot room in the summer may make kids want to leave before the session begins. Give your kids comfortable chairs, too.

10. Set the mood you want.

Peer counseling training should be fun! Learning takes place best in an atmosphere where one feels comfortable and at ease. You (assuming you will teach the class) should model the very behavior you want your kids to adopt. Specifically: everything shared in class will be kept confidential; no put-downs; the trainees are nonjudgmental; and there is support, caring, and love.

The director or person teaching the class sets the atmosphere and mood of the class. If he or she allows the trainees to get to know each other and bond, no one will want to miss a session.

SEVEN POINTS TO REMEMBER

• Be a facilitator, not a lecturer.
• Teach your kids with hands-on experiences, like *role-playing* (learners assume identities of others in a particular situation or dilemma and act accordingly), *sharing* (learners verbalize their

thoughts, feelings, and experiences to one or more peers), and *working in pairs or in threes*.

• Trainees learn from each other, not just from you.

• The mind can absorb only what the body can endure—take frequent breaks and allow trainees to stretch and walk around.

• Model the behavior you expect from your trainees—caring, listening, keeping confidentiality.

• Be relaxed and confident in class—this presupposes that you arrive well-prepared for the lesson.

• Stay flexible. Sometimes you'll have to put aside well-prepared lesson plans in order to give full attention to a student with a particular problem.

. . . AND STEPS TO SOLIDIFY THE PROGRAM

The importance of integrating the peer counseling program into the total church or parachurch program cannot be emphasized strongly enough. If the director and the peer counselors feel this is not happening, then it is their responsibility to make it happen.

The more the peer counseling program is integrated into church life as a whole, the more effective it will be. It may be a one-way street for a while, during which time the peer counseling program will do all the reaching out. But that's all right, for sooner or later others will see the value of peer counseling and will invite your participation in their departments.

Peer counseling should be an integral part of the total life of the church or parachurch organization. If it becomes isolated, communication with other departments breaks down, and the effectiveness of the program can be hindered.

• The director should attend all church staff meetings and report the effects of the peer counseling program on the congregation at large—especially when unchurched young people are brought into church because of the program.

• At church staff meetings the peer counseling director may hear of needs that can be met appropriately by the peer counselors, and recommend accordingly. Case in point: A pastor remarks in staff meeting that several divorcing parents are worried about their teenagers' reactions to the divorce. The director can naturally suggest that the peer counselors lead a support group for such teenagers.

• Ask all departments and ministries to pray regularly for peer counselors. Suggest to the counselors that they reciprocate with notes of appreciation as well as verbal thank-yous.

• Alert your peer counselors to other church programs with which they can integrate their counseling skills—visits to hospitals, convalescent homes, jails, homebound elderly, or senior centers are good opportunities.

• Remind your counselors to keep their eyes open for needs not being filled by their church, needs that could be filled by joining forces with another department of the church. Since the peer counselors are trained in cultural diversity, for instance, they may want to assist the Sunday school department in reaching more minorities.

Budget Worksheet

Administration (salaries—a portion of youth pastor's
  salary may be charged to peer counseling program) $_____

Supplies and materials (manuals and books) $_____

Professional consultation fees (if any) $_____

Operations/facilities $_____

Workshops/seminars/retreats $_____

Occasional honoraria (for guest speakers) $_____

Job Description:
Director of Peer Counseling

☐ Oversee and manage the peer counseling program.

☐ Promote and assure counselee confidentiality.

☐ Set up training sessions for beginning peer counselors. (The actual teaching of these classes may be delegated to another—a peer counseling consultant, for instance.)

☐ Provide supervision and on-going training for the advanced peer counselors. (This duty may also be delegated to a qualified person, but should be monitored by the director to assure quality and consistency.)

☐ Maintain accurate statistical records. (A yearly report should be given to the board of trustees and the pastor.)

☐ Provide and oversee the physical facilities used for peer counseling purposes.

☐ Help recruit new people for peer counseling training.

☐ Oversee the program's public relations within both the church and the community.

☐ Be available to support peer counselors in difficult situations and to consult with and make referrals to other mental health professionals when necessary.

☐ Interact with church staff concerning peer counseling matters.

SELECTING YOUR PEER COUNSELOR TRAINEES

I have fond memories of kids whom others considered unacceptable for peer counselor training. I remember the rugged young man with a Mohawk that was dyed jet black, except for the orange ends. It was Owen who tucked his vertical strip of hair into a Santa's cap one December afternoon and became the delight of a convalescent home Christmas party that the peer counseling class hosted. Owen hardly represented the norm at his conservative high school, but there were students who related to him in ways they did not relate to a typical kid. In other words, he helped the kids that the "good" students could not reach. The same was true of the handicapped girl, the recovering alcoholic, and the exchange student—each one a peer counselor, each one bringing a uniqueness to the class that made it exciting and interesting. Everyone learned from each other and came to accept people who were different from themselves.

I remember well-meaning teachers who came to me with names of "good students who would make excellent peer counselors." These teachers were surprised to see only a few of these "good students" selected, for the teachers—like many adults—believed that only leaders and exemplary youths make good peer counselors.

Those who criticize you for your selection of peer counselors may mean well, but they misunderstand the nature of peer counseling. If there are only certain kinds of kids who make good peer counselors, then only certain kinds of teenagers will be counseled. Remember that peer counselors go back to their own circles of friends, available to listen and help.

A solid peer counseling group has a cross-section of youths

from various ethnic, socioeconomic, and cultural backgrounds. It recruits youths with different personality types (introverts and extroverts), various levels of intellectual ability (F students as well as A students—and everyone in between), leaders and followers, emotionally healthy kids and those who bear the scars of dysfunctional homes, foreign exchange students and those who have never left their home state, active youth group members and those who attend only Sunday morning services.

Until your trainees listen to each other and appreciate each other's uniqueness, in their role as peer counselors they will be unlikely to accept and help teens who are different from themselves.

OPEN RECRUITING

Training sessions should be open to all youths in the church or organization. This does not mean that everyone who takes the training will become a designated peer counselor. After some young people have been through the sessions, they will decide peer counseling is not for them, or they will realize they do not have the time to pursue it. Or the group leader may determine that some people are not qualified, though they completed the training. (For example, although non-Christians may attend the training and be touched by the Lord, the final selection of peer counselors should include only Christian youths.) At the beginning of the sessions, of course, make it very clear that completing the training does not necessarily qualify one for counseling. The leader should make it equally clear, however, that the training is valuable in itself, for it can equip students with skills for living, whether or not the teenager functions as a designated peer counselor.

Training classes should be conducted often enough during the year to squeeze in everyone who wants to attend. More than one class a year accommodates new young people moving into the community as well as those wishing to repeat the sessions because of absenteeism in a previous session.

THE APPLICATION PROCESS

After you've selected a director and possibly a supervisor and trained them in peer counseling (or while a consultant is training them), announce to your kids that you are accepting applications from those who want to be trained as peer counselors. Announce it orally in Sunday school classes and at youth meetings, and in writing in the church bulletin and in newsletters. Use the application form (see p. 54) or a simple sign-up sheet.

If more teenagers apply than there's room for in the program, select your twenty or twenty-five not by a first-come-first-served process, but by personal interview—for you want a cross section of your organization or church, with different ethnic, socioeconomic, cultural backgrounds, and personalities represented.

Don't choose only your leaders. A peer counseling program needs introverts as well as extroverts. One of the outcomes of the class will be that young people will get to know others whom they have not talked to before, often thinking of these peers as being different from themselves.

Chances are, you won't need to solicit trainees for a second class, because the first group will spread the word—and probably deliver a fairly good cross-section of students the next time, too.

The application process itself has its critics, however. Some feel that it deters some kids from applying. Furthermore, of the kids who do apply, some of these are not accepted to training. So two groups—those who didn't apply and those who applied but weren't accepted—may be eliminated before they had the slimmest opportunity to quite possibly become excellent peer counselors. I've found that some youths who were not considered likely peer counselor candidates at the beginning of the sessions turn out to be skilled, sensitive, and caring people when given the opportunity to develop and mature in the classes.

PARENT CONSENT LETTER

Make certain that each trainee has a parent permission letter signed. If you met with the parents after the trainee selection was complete, you probably asked the parents to sign the letter at that time. There are usually absentee parents, however, and you may have mailed their letters to them. Check your files to make certain all the letters have been received before the first training session.

If you did not have a parent meeting, or plan to have it immediately before or after the first session, have your letters ready to give to the parents at that time. **Be sure to double-check this consent letter with your organization's local legal counsel or lawyer before using it.**

A sample of a parent consent letter can be found on p. 55.

SELECTION OF THE PEER COUNSELORS

After the trainees complete the course, it's up to you to select the designated peer counselors from among the trainees. Sometimes the entire group may be chosen; other times, all but a few are selected. Keep in mind that one of the benefits to the trainee is the feeling of belonging to the group. Consequently, the leader may choose to invite *all* members to the advanced training, even though all will not function as peer counselors at the time. Once a trainee has been chosen to be a peer counselor, the confidentiality contract (see p. 56) should be signed and turned in.

Base your selection of peer counselors on **your need, their skills,** and **their personal qualities.**

1. **Need.** How many designated peer counselors are already in service? How many more are needed? Some leaders place no limit on the number of peer counselors who are serving at one time; other leaders want only a certain number, with alternate trained peer counselors available to step in if someone should move away or decide to go on inactive status.

2. **Skills.** Some leaders score the progress of trainees' skills during role-playing in class (see the "Role-Play Evaluation Sheet" on pp. 57–58). Some leaders do not consider trainees competent until they have demonstrated proficiency according to these scores. Other leaders feel this method of selection is ineffective

50

and unfair. They doubt that skill level actually reveals the most effective peer counselors, believing instead that skill level is only part of what makes an effective peer counselor. Caring, available time, commitment, and Christian love are just as important.

3. Personal qualities. Selecting trainees with the combination of skills, desire, commitment, personal relationship to Christ, concern, and caring is the ideal. But few trainees have ideal amounts of each quality. Some have less of some and more of others. Admit freely to the trainees that the selection process is subjective and based on several factors. For their part, leaders must remember that peer counseling training is meant to encourage youths, not discourage them. Trainees who do not qualify to be peer counselors need to be told privately what areas they need to improve. Give them hope for becoming a peer counselor later, unless there are specific reasons to the contrary.

When the training classes are completed, use this checklist to help you weigh trainees' skills and traits so that you can choose wisely who will be your active counselors.[1] Remember that your teenagers are still growing and maturing and may need more time in certain areas. This checklist is presented as a standard, *not* as a mandatory requirement.

CHECKLIST
CRITERIA FOR SELECTING COUNSELORS

• **Spiritual maturity.** The peer counselor should be a Christian with an active relationship with God. This includes a regular prayer life. He or she should also have some knowledge of Scripture and understanding in applying Scripture to life.

• **Psychological stability.** The peer counselor should be psychologically stable, not emotionally volatile, but open and vulnerable. He or she should not be suffering from a serious psychological disorder.

• **Love for and interest in people.** The peer counselor should be a warm, caring, and genuine person with a sincere interest in people and their welfare.

- **Spiritual gifts.** The peer counselor should possess spiritual gifts suitable for counseling, such as exhortation, mercy, discernment of spirits, knowledge, wisdom, and healing.
- **Life experience.** Although young people may not have experienced a broad range of life events, some will have come from dysfunctional families, witnessed the death of a family member or friend, known the pain of alcohol or drug abuse, or even been the victim of child abuse.
- **Previous training or experience in helping people.** Experience is helpful but not necessary for the peer counselor to have.
- **Age, sex, education, socioeconomic status, and ethnic/ cultural background.** It is helpful for a variety of peer backgrounds and ages, as well as both sexes, to be represented on the peer counseling team.
- **Availability and teachability.** The peer counselor should have the time to be trained, supervised, and involved in a peer counseling program. He or she should be teachable and open to learning a biblical approach to helping people.
- **Ability to maintain confidentiality.** The peer counselor should be able to maintain confidentiality and protect the privacy of counselees. This should be done by following appropriate guidelines, including limits to confidentiality (see Chapter Six, p. 60).

REPLACEMENT AND ROTATION

Because members of youth groups have various commitments to work and school at different times in the year, some peer counselors can serve for only a few months. Others may want to remain active indefinitely. You'll need to have a plan for replacing and rotating your peer counselors as circumstances call for it.

Replacement. A teenager may want to be a peer counselor for a year, and then go on inactive status. Although this student may still attend all the meetings and advanced training classes, counselees will not be assigned to him or her. Consequently, the leader must replace this person with an active peer counselor. Other youths may find they must drop out of the program entirely because of moving away, changing jobs or work schedules, or electing to do Christian service in another ministry of the church. You'll need training sessions at least twice a year so that the supply of peer counselors never diminishes.

Rotation. A peer counselor may elect to be on active status for one year, inactive the next, and then return to active the following year. The time period for this type of rotation may be six months instead of a year. A value of rotation is that more people get to serve as peer counselors. There is also the benefit of lessening the chance of burnout. Not all peer counselors, however, will want to be involved in a rotation schedule, and the idea of having veteran peer counselors serve year after year has merit.

Cliques. Youths who are selected as peer counselors must remember they are chosen to *serve*, and in true Christian service there is no room for cliques to be formed. The peer counselors need to keep Colossians 3:23–24 in mind: "Whatever you do, work at it with all your heart, as working for the Lord, not for men. . . . It is the Lord Christ you are serving."

Application Form for
Peer Counseling Program

Name: _____

Address: _____

_____

Age: _____ Phone: _____

Year in school (circle one):
     freshman   sophomore   junior   senior   out-of-school

Name of your school and/or workplace: _____

1. Why do you want to be a peer counselor?

2. What does being a Christian mean to you personally?

3. List the groups to which you belong, both in and out of school:

4. List the qualifications you have that you think would make you a good peer counselor:

5. Describe any previous counseling experiences you have had (for example, summer camp counselor):

6. If you want, comment on anything else about yourself that you might like us to know:

Parent Consent Letter

Dear Parent,

   Your son/daughter has made application and been selected to participate in a peer counseling training course at _____ church (or parachurch organization). The sessions are scheduled from _____ until _____ every _____. Training sessions begin _____ and run through _____ (_____ weeks).

   This training course is designed to help your teenager learn how to help other young people. Skills taught in the class include learning how to be a good listener, how to communicate with others effectively, and how to help others work out their own problems.

   Later on, in advanced training, trainees also learn to examine their own feelings and values in the areas of crisis counseling, family, drug issues, sexuality, death and loss, pregnancy, spiritual issues, peer pressure, AIDS, eating disorders, school problems, suicide, codependency, cults, the occult, child abuse, and war.

   As part of the advanced training course, your son/daughter will be given the opportunity to help a peer. In all cases, trainees will be closely supervised by an adult leader.

   During a training session a questionnaire on self-esteem or attitude may be given to the trainees. All information will be kept private and will not be shared with anyone without your permission.

   If you agree that your son or daughter can participate in the peer counseling training program, please sign below and return the letter to the church or parachurch organization.

   Please contact me if you have any questions. You are welcome to visit the training class or to examine any of the course materials. Thank you for your cooperation.

Sincerely,

_____   _____
(Leader's signature)   (Leader's phone number)

- -

I give my consent for _____ , my son or daughter, to be in the peer counseling class at _____ church/parachurch organization.

_____   _____
(Parent's signature)   (Date)

Confidentiality Contract

Date_____

As a peer counselor, I will be involved in conversations of an extremely confidential nature. I understand that I must not divulge any of the information that I gain through peer counseling. An exception to this is sharing with the peer counseling leader and the peer counselors in my class when case studies are being discussed for supervision purposes, keeping names anonymous. I understand also that the following situations are exceptions to maintaining confidentiality: (1) child or elder abuse; (2) danger to self; or (3) danger to others.

_____
Trainee's Signature

_____
Leader's Signature

Role-Play Evaluation Sheet

Counselor: _____ **Counselee:** _____
Date: _____

Instructions: Observe the trainee's behaviors carefully during the role-play. Check the space to the left of each criterion if you observe it. Use the spaces to the right for any comments you want to make.

☐ Maintains good eye contact. _____
_____

☐ Is attentive. _____
_____

☐ Sits in a relaxed manner. _____
_____

☐ Uses appropriate gestures (helpful nods and smiles). _____
_____

☐ Accurately restates the counselee's most important thoughts and feelings. _____
_____

☐ Paces his or her responses. _____
_____

☐ Asks probing questions to gain more information without making the counselee feel uncomfortable. _____
_____

☐ Asks open-ended questions. _____
_____

☐ Is open and nondefensive. _____

_____

☐ Uses "I" statements. _____

_____

☐ Is comfortable with silence. _____

_____

☐ Shows warmth and empathy. _____

_____

☐ Is patient. _____

_____

☐ Provides helpful feedback. _____

_____

☐ Encourages counselee to take appropriate action. _____

_____

☐ Makes appropriate referrals. _____

_____

☐ Uses prayer and the Scriptures appropriately. _____

_____

☐ Designs follow-up plans. _____

_____

☐ Listens for camouflaged feelings when necessary. _____

_____

☐ Is accepting and nonjudgmental. _____

_____

DYNAMICS OF THE PEER COUNSELOR-COUNSELEE RELATIONSHIP

Tony was warm, understanding, and a good listener who gave freely of his time to anyone in the youth group who needed it. Yet precisely because he knew he was an effective peer counselor, he was perplexed and disappointed with the lack of progress in his counseling with Rita.

He had known Rita as an acquaintance in church for a few years, but Tony had never noticed how attractive she was until he served as her peer counselor. He soon found himself looking forward to spending an hour each week with the perky, vivacious redhead. He wasn't even bothered at first by a gradual inability to listen carefully to Rita's problems. Tony soon realized that he was allowing his mind to wander . . . Rita *was* pretty . . . maybe she'd go out with him . . . what a date *that* would be. . . . Tony had never encountered this problem with past counselees, and for the moment his previous training in counselor-counselee relationship dynamics slipped his mind.

Weeks passed before Tony finally admitted to himself and to his peer counseling supervisor that he had gone over the boundary of an appropriate peer counseling relationship with Rita. He had allowed himself to become infatuated with her and was no longer an effective peer counselor. With the help of his supervisor, Tony was able eventually to end the peer counseling relationship with Rita and refer her to another peer counselor who helped her in a more appropriate way.

Tony's dilemma is common when counselors or their counselees misunderstand their roles. In particular, peer counselors must clearly understand the relationship between themselves and their counselees before they are commissioned.

FIRST CONTACT WITH THE COUNSELEE

The peer counselor reaches out to the counselee by introducing himself or herself in a friendly manner and initiating conversation. During this first meeting, the peer counselor lets the counselee know in what ways he or she may be able to help. The counselor makes it very clear that he or she will listen and assist, but will not directly solve the counselee's problem. The counselee will do that for himself or herself—with help, of course, from the peer counselor.

The first meeting may be awkward for the counselee, but such relationships usually become more comfortable as the meetings continue. Confidentiality and its limits should be discussed at the initial meeting so trust can begin to form and misunderstandings can be avoided.

THE ROLE OF THE PEER COUNSELOR

• The peer counselor's primary responsibility is to the counselee. Peer counselors respect their counselees' integrity and guard their welfare throughout the counseling relationship.
• The peer counselor keeps all information that the counselee divulges during counseling sessions in strict confidence. Counselees are told that there are only three exceptions to the confidentiality rule: when there is clear and imminent danger to the counselee (suicide); when there is clear and imminent danger to another (homicide); and when there is any report of child abuse or elder abuse. The counselee will also be told that although his or her identity will not be revealed, the peer counselor may need to review the counselee's problems with the supervisor of the peer counseling program and possibly with fellow peer counselors in the supervisory group. Material shared in supervisory sessions is confidential (excluding the three exceptions already discussed).

Knowing when to tell a supervisor is as critical as holding a confidence. I remember a peer counselor who observed bruise marks on a girl's face, arms, and legs. When asked about them, the counselee said that she had fallen off her horse, but later broke down and started crying when her father's name entered the conversation. She then confessed that her father had come home drunk and had beaten both her and her mother. The girl became hysterical when told that the incident had to be reported. She said her mother would kill herself if it was known that her husband beat her. The counselee said that she didn't care about herself, but she felt she must protect her mother. She said that she had promised her mother she wouldn't tell anyone, and now she felt very guilty for talking about it.

The peer counselor knew she had to report the child abuse, but she was afraid of what might happen to the mother if she did. Yet she went ahead and talked to her supervisor, who assured her that she had done the correct thing. (At times like these, one sees the importance of having a supervisor available.) The supervisor did the actual reporting to the authorities, and the peer counselor remained in close contact with the counselee.

Peer counselors must be reminded often that reporting is not a choice—it is the law. And although the counselee might feel better momentarily if the incident is not reported, that act of "kindness" might leave the door open to a future fatal beating.
• Peer counselors should be involved in an ongoing program for updating knowledge and improving skills.
• When peer counselors observe symptoms or problems that are beyond their competence, they must refer the counselee to a professional.
• Peer counselors should participate in regular supervision that affords them the opportunity for case consultation and improvement of counseling skills. These supervisory opportunities may take place during the advanced classes of the peer counseling training course.
• Peer counselors need a safe, lockable file cabinet or drawer where written notes pertaining to their counselees can be kept.

• Peer counselors need to keep themselves in good physical, mental, and spiritual health.

• Peer counselors should arrange a meeting place that provides privacy, security, and a degree of comfort for their counselees.

• Peer counselors should state their desire to help and be available to their counselees.

THE ROLE OF THE COUNSELEE

• Counselees need to be truthful when talking about their problems and issues.

• Counselees need to be punctual for appointments and will always let their counselors know ahead of time if they must cancel a session.

• A counselee may terminate the counseling at any time or ask to be referred to another peer counselor or to a professional therapist, a pastor, or a residential treatment center.

ESTABLISHING TRUST

If significant trust is to be cultivated, a counselee must know that what he or she divulges to a counselor will be kept in confidence (with the exceptions detailed previously). In other words, there should be no surprises for counselees after they've shared information with their peer counselors.

Even after a counselor explains the circumstances that by law *must* be reported to authorities, a teenage counselee may mention abuse of some sort—but then beg the counselor to not report it. Prepare your peer counselors for this possibility, and plan with them how to respond.

Besides confidentiality, counselors can establish trust by discussing with their counselees how often they will meet. Usually once a week is adequate; in a crisis situation, however, more frequent meetings can be necessary. Arranging a regular meeting goes beyond mere scheduling. It assures a teenager that a counselor will be there for him or her, as someone to call on for help, a steady shoulder on which to lean.

BOUNDARIES

As in any relationship, there are boundaries that should not be crossed. This applies to both the peer counselor and the counselee.

A peer counselor may be tempted to know more and more about whatever is evolving in the life of the counselee, especially if it is shocking news. The counselee, of course, has a right to disclose only the information that pertains to the immediate problem, and the counselor should respect that right to privacy.

Nor should the counselee cross certain boundaries. A counselee may want to dump not only a problem on the peer counselor, but all responsibility for solving it, too. A counselor should neither assume full responsibility for solving the counselee's problem nor feel guilty if things do not work out as planned.

FIVE HINDRANCES TO A HEALTHY COUNSELOR-COUNSELEE RELATIONSHIP

1. Rescuing. It can be easy for a peer counselor to do something for the counselee that he or she shouldn't because the counselor has experience the counselee lacks. Maybe the peer counselor thinks that the counselee is immobilized by the problem and honestly cannot take steps for himself or herself. Or maybe a counselor likes the feeling of making things turn out right for someone. Whatever the reason, *a peer counselor should not rescue.* By rescuing, the counselee gets the message that he or she can't handle the problem. Rescuers remove responsibility from their counselees, and the counselees do not learn from the experience. The next time a problem comes along, a counselee is no better prepared to solve the problem than the first time.

Evelyn thought she was helping Oliver when she told him the exact words to use whenever he had a problem communicating with his family members. Once, for instance, he followed her advice to the letter and convinced his mother to allow him to go away for a weekend with friends. Later he had a problem with his younger sister and asked Evelyn what exactly to say to her in order to resolve the conflict. She advised him in detail what to say and do. The following week Oliver asked her what to say to his best friend with whom he had just had a misunderstanding.

At this point, Evelyn finally realized that she was a rescuer, not a peer counselor. She had unwittingly made Oliver dependent on her instead of helping him shape his own problem-solving and communication skills. She stopped solving his problems and began helping him explore his own solutions.

Also, if the rescue effort fails, the counselee may not entrust another problem to the counselor (or to any other counselor) and thus have no help to solve the problem. Rescuing takes its toll on counselors, too, for they likely feel guilty and inadequate for not being able to make it all work out like they think it should.

An exception, however: Occasionally a counselee is truly immobilized or so disturbed that the peer counselor must *intervene directly*—in obtaining emergency medical or psychiatric help, for example. When the counselee is severely depressed or psychotic (with bizarre symptoms of hallucinations and/or delusions) or has overdosed on drugs or is seriously suicidal, the peer counselor must intervene.

2. Overdoing advice. Don't overdo the role of advice giver or problem solver. Some counselors tend to get on a power trip, enjoying having others look to them for the answers. They become controllers, and the counselees become controlled. Even though some counselees actually want someone to tell them what to do, most will not remain in a controlling relationship for very long.

Giving advice or feedback and helping the counselee to problem solve are appropriate interventions for peer counselors to engage in at times, but peer counselors need to be careful to not overuse such interventions and to concentrate primarily on listening, understanding, and providing support. A Christian peer counselor may have to plainly advise a counselee dealing with, say, promiscuous premarital sex. Yet even though a Christian peer counselor will uphold biblical values, the final decision is still the counselee's—and the peer counselor should respect his or her freedom to choose.

3. Excessive emotional involvement. Either the counselor or the counselee may get snared by this. One of them finds the other warm, fun to be with, someone that would be nice to have as a friend. Peer counselors must understand that though this may happen quite naturally, the relationship between the two will change. They will become buddies who share things rather than having a counselor-counselee relationship, in which the counselor is objective.

4. Sexual attraction. He listens. He's interested in what she says. She's never met a guy who's so warm and compassionate. She realizes that she looks forward to the meetings for reasons other than just working on her problem.

Or: A male counselee sees the same caring qualities in his female peer counselor that he so admires in his own mother. He gradually begins thinking of her as a potential date.

It would be wrong to say that a peer counselor should never let counseling lead to a dating relationship because, quite frankly, it will happen sometimes. I know at least one happily married couple who first met in a peer counselor-counselee relationship. If two people find themselves attracted to each other and want to date, however, they should terminate the peer counseling relationship, and the counselee should be referred to another peer counselor.

5. Feelings of inadequacy when a problem isn't "solved." Some kids are devastated when they cannot achieve a "successful" solution to a problem. Students successful in school or in other areas of their lives have a difficult time handling what they consider failure.

You need to spend time during training sessions explaining the true nature of what may look at first to be a failure. Students should know up front that things won't always work out as they hope when working with a counselee. Point out to them that even professional counselors do not have a 100 percent success rate; they know the frustrations of failures, too. Nor should the necessity of referring a counselee make them feel like a failure. Serving as a bridge to a professional or other counselor is *always* a success. Remind your teen counselors that sometimes it is only *because* they refer, that counselees will get the help they need.

CULTURAL DIVERSITY IN PEER COUNSELING

avid, a Caucasian high school peer counselor in a church youth group, was trying to help Jim, a Chinese-American teenager. David realized that Jim's family and cultural background were quite different from his own. Jim struggled with trying to live up to his parents' straight-A expectations so that he could make it to medical school after college. No matter how hard he has tried, however, Jim earned only a B average—and his parents were upset. Jim was actually uninterested in medical school, but didn't know how to tell his parents. So David initially encouraged Jim to assert himself and talk directly and openly to his parents, but Jim resisted, telling David that such assertions were inappropriate in Chinese culture, where respect for parents and elders is valued. Direct confrontation of parents, especially by a teenager, is deemed inappropriate. Jim loved his parents and did not want to hurt them, but on the other hand, he felt stressed out and a little depressed about not fulfilling their expectations.

One day David read an article about *indirectly* helping kids from Asian cultures who have academic and career problems with parents who have high expectations. The article recommended enlisting the aid of a respected uncle or grandfather in the family, who could talk to the parents more directly and effectively than a young person could.

During their next peer counseling session, David asked Jim if he had another relative—an uncle he especially liked, maybe—who would mediate for him by talking to his parents on his behalf about his grades and career options. To David's surprise and delight, Jim thought his mother's brother could do that, since he visited with Jim often and they got along well together.

His uncle proved to be very understanding and helpful. He gently mentioned to Jim's parents that he was a good and hard-working boy who might make a better accountant or business-man (careers that Jim was genuinely interested in) than a medical doctor. Jim's parents eventually listened to him about other career options and became more reasonable in their expectations about his grades.

Peer counseling trainers need to understand other ethnic groups and cultures themselves for their peer counselors to be effective. If at all possible, therefore, peer counseling classes should have a cultural cross-section of trainees—especially in communities composed of many nationalities. Students listen and learn from peers who are different from themselves. As they learn to accept and appreciate other cultures, their attitudes change and stereotypes fall away. By the time the training is complete, the peer counselors are then prepared to help coun-selees from diverse cultures.

Although ethnic and cultural diversity is not uniformly present in every city, it is growing across more cities and states. American society is becoming more culturally diverse and plural-istic—due in part to heavy Hispanic and Asian immigration. Some of the material in this chapter may not be as relevant to peer counselors in parts of the country that are still predomi-nantly Caucasian. It is helpful, nevertheless, for all peer coun-selors to know something about people of other cultural and ethnic groups. Such cross-cultural knowledge can help peer counselors be more sensitive, understanding, flexible, and broad-minded—and therefore be more effective helpers of peers from different cultures or ethnic groups.

This chapter's material is crucial for peer counselors in cities that abound with cultural and ethnic diversity. These peer coun-selors will sooner or later find themselves helping peers of other nationalities or ethnic groups.

WHAT DOES THE BIBLE SAY ABOUT CROSS-CULTURAL COUNSELING?

You may think first of the apostle Paul who, though he was a Jew, was called to preach the gospel to the Gentiles. Because his letters to believers scattered throughout the Middle East often took the form of counseling, Paul could be thought of as a cross-cultural counselor.

> Though I am free and belong to no man, I make myself a slave to everyone, to win as many as possible. To the Jews I became like a Jew, to win the Jews. To those under the law I became like one under the law (though I myself am not under the law), so as to win those under the law. To those not having the law I became like one not having the law (though I am not free from God's law but am under Christ's law), so as to win those not having the law. To the weak I became weak, to win the weak. I have become all things to all men so that by all possible means I might save some (1 Cor. 9:19–22).

The first-century deacon Philip may also have been a cross-cultural counselor.

> Now an angel of the Lord said to Philip, "Go south to the road—the desert road—that goes down from Jerusalem to Gaza." So he started out, and on his way he met an Ethiopian eunuch, an important official in charge of all the treasury of Candace, queen of the Ethiopians. This man had gone to Jerusalem to worship, and on his way home was sitting in his chariot reading the book of Isaiah the prophet. The Spirit told Philip, "Go to that chariot and stay near it." Then Philip ran up to the chariot and heard the man reading Isaiah the prophet. "Do you understand what you are reading?" Philip asked. "How can I," he said, "unless someone explains it to me?" So he invited Philip to come up and sit with him (Acts 8:26–31).

The subsequent conversation led to the Ethiopian's conversion and baptism. Philip and the Ethiopian came from different countries and had different backgrounds, but one man clearly had a problem and the other helped.

Finally, in Christ's Great Commission he clearly directs Christians to cross cultural boundaries and to minister to those who are different from themselves—to go out to all nations and tell them the Good News.

> "Therefore go and make disciples of all nations, baptizing them in the name of the Father and of the Son and of the Holy Spirit, and teaching them to obey everything I have commanded you. And surely I am with you always, to the very end of the age" (Matt. 28:19–20).

Urban American Christians, however, have only to open their front doors to see that nations have come to them. What an impact Christians can have on these people if we seek to understand their background and reach out to meet their needs. Peer counseling in Christian youth groups is a natural place to begin this worthwhile work.

Yet peer counselors must be trained to do this work. In *Counseling Cross-Culturally,* author David J. Hesselgrave states,

> Increasingly, professional and lay Christians are being presented with the opportunity to help and even heal people from other cultures. Most Christian workers with extensive intercultural experience will admit that they have often lacked the ability to relate to problems and perplexities occasioned by cultural differences. Yet training in cross-cultural counseling per se is minimal at best and often nonexistent.[1]

The need is present for cross-cultural training, and peer counseling leaders cannot leave it out of the training sessions.

CULTURAL SIMILARITIES

If your peer counselors are to be effective in cross-cultural counseling, they need to understand the similarities as well as the differences between races and nationalities. Norman D. Sundberg states,

> At the heart of research on intercultural counseling is the problem of similarities and differences. One fact is that human beings around the world share many similarities, such as the ability to interbreed, the presence of physical environments, and the common experiences of birth, early helplessness, growing up, and growing old. Another fact is that human beings share many things with their groups of identification, though not with all mankind—knowledge of specific places, ways of

socializing the young, language, and expectations about authority. Finally, each human being is unique, having one-of-a-kind fingerprints, a special history, and a particular life style. The counselor meeting a client for the first time encounters all three aspects in one person—the universal, the group-specific, and the unique. The counselor also has these tripartite characteristics. Furthermore, the counseling pair also meets in a context, an interaction in a social and physical setting, which has a history and relation with similar contexts.[2]

The effectiveness of your peer counselors' cross-cultural counseling depends upon their ability to correctly identify and interpret universal, group-specific, and idiosyncratic factors that both the peer counselor and the counselee bring to the counseling situation. It is the similarity between human beings that makes identification, understanding, and empathy possible. If there were no similarities, counseling would be impossible.

WHAT COUNSELORS MUST KNOW ABOUT CULTURAL DISTINCTIVES

General descriptions of cultural or ethnic groups are just that—general. A particular member of a specific group may not carry certain general characteristics of that group because of his or her *degree of acculturation* to mainstream Caucasian culture in this country. A third-generation Chinese-American who is well acculturated into mainstream Caucasian culture, for example, is more like a typical Caucasian or white American than, say, an elderly and recent Chinese immigrant from Asia who speaks mainly, or only, Chinese. In cross-cultural counseling it is essential to note and respect individual differences, even within a particular ethnic group.

The following general information is intended to help you and your counselors understand their counselees better, not to cause stereotyping.

White Western

In *Innovative Approaches to Counseling*, Gary Collins points out that white Westerners have distinctive attitudes and behaviors, including their

- **Attitudes toward time.** We adhere to rigid time schedules, disapprove of wasting time, and are very much controlled by the clock.
- **Personal habits.** We make direct eye contact, rarely hug, tend to control our emotions, wash our hands frequently, almost never spit in public, shower every day, eat with utensils instead of our fingers, and rarely have animals in the house, except a cat or dog.
- **Views of the family.** We value youths rather than family elders, emphasize the nuclear family rather than an extended family of numerous relatives, tend to be informal at home, and are open in expressing our feelings to family members.
- **Perspectives on individual achievement.** We believe in rugged individualism, assume that people should take responsibility for their own lives, emphasize the importance of education and the drive for success, value autonomy, and reward those who are assertive and hard working.[3]

Collins continues, "Most of us assume that English is the best language, that science is the most effective way to gain knowledge about the natural world, that democracy (as we define it) is the best freedom from government and other external controls, that free enterprise is the superior system of economics, and that counselees can get better if they are determined to do so. We tend to believe that our culture is the most advanced, the most correct, and the most Christian."[4]

Such assumptions and beliefs are not all necessarily valid or true, of course.

In *Counseling the Culturally Different*,[5] Derald Sue gives us some informative summaries of ethnic and racial groups your peer counselors should be familiar with.

Asian

- Being patriarchal, the father is traditionally the head of the household, and his authority is unquestioned. The primary duty of the son is to be a good son, and even his obligations to be a good husband or father come second to his duty as a son.
- The dominant orientation of Asian families has always been

conservative and resistant to change.

• The roles of family members are rigidly defined, allowing for few significant deviations. Conflicts within the family are minimized because the structure is so arranged that roles do not interfere with others.

• Built into the family relationships are strong values that stress approaching problems subtly and indirectly rather than openly.

• Asians typically expend much effort to avoid offending others.

• The welfare and integrity of the family is of great importance. Members of the family are expected to submerge behaviors and feelings to further the welfare of the family and its reputation.

• Parents constantly emphasize their sons' and daughters' obligations to the family. If children attempt to act independently, contrary to the wishes of the parents, parents usually tell them that they are selfish, inconsiderate, and ungrateful for all their parents have done for them.

• Because of their characteristic formality in interpersonal relations, Asians can be uncomfortable relating to the much more informal and spontaneous nature of Westerners.

• Asian culture tends to be a "shame" culture, in that failures that may have nothing to do with the individual's efforts tend to be internalized.

African-American

• African-American culture has a strong oral tradition of storytelling as a means of expressing and preserving its philosophy.

• Humor is an important part of the oral tradition.

• An appreciation of music and dance has also been a part of African-American culture. The spirituals, the blues, jazz, and soul music have generally been forms of expression for African-Americans' feelings.

• African-Americans scrutinize the nonverbal behavior of individuals and its cultural connotations. They are apt to spend much time observing people to see "where they're coming from."

• African-Americans do not necessarily look one another in the eye to communicate. They can carry on a lively conversation and yet busy their hands and eyes elsewhere.

• African-American culture is people-oriented rather than thing-oriented. It emphasizes humanism. Few black women give up for adoption their babies born out of wedlock. Instead, all African-American children are treated equally, with little regard for the legitimacy of their birth.

• African-American families lack rigid, sex-linked roles. Both men and women may share in household responsibilities, the caring of children, and work outside the home.

• African-American culture values an extended-family kinship system, especially as a supportive and therapeutic base. It is within this family system that individual members work out personal problems.

Hispanic

• Hispanic culture carries a strong sense of the extended family.

• Most Hispanics are bicultural in the sense that they are members of both the Anglo and Hispanic cultures, but there is great variation in their commitment to either the Anglo or the Hispanic culture.

• Hispanics are a significantly undereducated group, compared both to the general population and to African-Americans, as measured by median years of education, percentage with five or less years of school, and graduation from high school.

• Hispanic culture is an aggregate of distinct subcultures, each emanating from a different geographic area; Hispanics, therefore, can be quite different from each other.

Native American

• Native Americans believe that Mother Earth gives birth and sustains life for all living creatures. They do not make the marked contrast between humans and animals that others do.

• Happiness is very important to Native Americans. They feel life is to be enjoyed and people should be able to laugh at misery.

• Native Americans believe learning comes through legends; knowledge comes by remembering great stories of the past.

• Humility is important to the Native Americans, causing them to be passive-aggressive, gentle head hangers, and very modest.

• A Native American's tribe and extended family come before self.

• Native American culture has a history of art. They believe people should live with their hands. Manual activity is sacred.

• All religions, all things, and all living creatures fit into the "Hoop of Life." They are all part of a Native American's respect for everything—including all religions.

FEELINGS OF THE CROSS-CULTURAL COUNSELEE

Needless to say, a culturally different counselee assigned to a peer counselor may be anxious about ethnic, racial, or cultural differences. Past and continuing discrimination against the culturally different may cause minority counselees to guard their real feelings. Author Sue states: "Suspicion, apprehension, verbal constriction, unnatural reactions, open resentment and hostility, and 'passive' or 'cool' behaviors may all be expressed. Self-disclosure and the possible establishment of a working relationship can be seriously delayed and/or prevented from occurring. In all cases, the counselor may be put to severe tests about his/her trustworthiness. A culturally effective counselor is one who is able to adequately resolve challenges to his/her credibility."[6]

For example, an African-American counselee is very quiet during an initial counseling session. The Caucasian counselor may interpret that quietness as defensiveness—when actually the counselee is behaving in an appropriate, cautious way, waiting to decide whether to trust the counselor.

If peer counselors are forewarned that their trustworthiness (sincerity, openness, honesty, or motivation) may be put to the test, they are better prepared to handle the situation. Although most peer counselors consider themselves trustworthy, minority counselees may require proof. "First, the minority client is likely to constantly test the counselor regarding issues of confidentiality," Sue warns. "Second, the onus of responsibility for proving trustworthiness falls on the counselor. Third, to prove one is trustworthy requires, at times, self-disclosure on the part of the counselor."[7]

Even if a counselee is convinced of a counselor's trustworthiness, the counselee may yet question (verbally or nonverbally) the other's ability to help. Although peer counselors are certainly not experts, they are trained to listen and give support. Counselees must feel that their counselors recognize their own limitations and have the knowledge and skills to refer the counselee to a professional when the situation warrants it.

Just as counselors must understand their different-cultured counselees' demands for trustworthiness and ability, so must they understand and accept their worldviews—how they perceive their relationship to nature, to institutions, to other people, to other things. Worldviews are simply attitudes, values, opinions, and concepts that affect thought, decision making, behavior, and events. A peer counselor must not only realize that his or her worldviews are not necessarily those of the counselee, but must also understand the worldview of the counselee.

FEELINGS OF THE CROSS-CULTURAL COUNSELOR

Peer counselors may feel as anxious, awkward, and frustrated as their cross-cultural counselees. So after acknowledging those feelings, peer counselors of the differently cultured should—

• Be vulnerable and ask the counselee questions about his or her culture that the peer counselor does not know about or understand.

• Listen and empathize with the counselee.

• Talk to friends from the counselee's culture in order to understand the culture better.

• Read relevant literature about the counselee's culture, as well as literature on effective cross-cultural counseling.

• Attend workshops on cross-cultural counseling.

EFFECTIVE CROSS-CULTURAL COUNSELING

Peer counselors who have had some experience know that

each counselee is unique. They also know that each counseling situation is different from all others, and that they must adjust to each new situation. Being rigid can lead to ineffective counseling. Peer counselors will want to continue to improve and grow in their cross-cultural counseling skills, and they will also need to learn to handle their own feelings when counseling someone from another culture. The following characteristics of an effective cross-cultural counselor are, of course, ideal.[8] New peer counselors should not be discouraged if they do not possess all of them. However, we have found that they will be helpful in cross-cultural counseling situations.

Cross-cultural counseling is most effective when

• The counselor shares or understands the counselee's worldview. Although the counselor does not need to accept and agree with the counselee's perspectives, values, beliefs, and attitudes, the effective counselor attempts to see the world as the counselee sees it.

• The culturally skilled counselor has moved from cultural ignorance to recognizing his or her own cultural baggage and sees other cultures as equally valuable as his or her own.

• The counselor is comfortable with differences that exist in race, beliefs, expectations, social backgrounds, and attitudes, yet without professing "color-blindness" or denying differences that exist in attitudes and beliefs. Regardless of color or other physical differences, each individual is equally human.

• Culturally skilled counselors understand the sociopolitical system's operation in the United States with respect to its treatment of minorities, as well as the impact and operation of oppression (racism, sexism), the politics of counseling, and the racist concepts that have permeated the mental health helping professions.

• The counselor understands and uses culturally appropriate communication skills, sending and receiving verbal and nonverbal messages accurately and appropriately. And because communication is a two-way process, the culturally skilled counselor must be able to read (receive) messages from the counselee. This requires that the peer counselor must understand the counselee's language, gestures, and slang expressions. It is important to understand what counselees think about direct eye contact (many cultural groups avoid this), tone of voice, rate of speech, talking about intimate issues, appropriate distance between people when they talk, use of titles, and other issues that may be different from the counselor's expectations.

• The counselor is flexible and sensitive to cultural differences. According to Sue, "Studies have consistently revealed that (a) economically and educationally disadvantaged clients may not be oriented toward 'talk therapy'; (b) self-disclosure may be incompatible with cultural values of Asian-Americans, Chicanos, and Native Americans; (c) the sociopolitical atmosphere may dictate against self-disclosure; (d) the ambiguous nature of counseling may be antagonistic to life values of the minority client, and (e) many minority clients prefer an active/directive approach to an inactive/nondirective one in counseling."[9]

As David Augsburger states in *Pastoral Counseling across Cultures,* "Culturally aware counselors see themselves as universal citizens, related to all humans as well as distinct from all of them. They live in the world, not just their own community or country. Aware as they are of what is culture-bound and class-bound, they refuse to allow what is local to be valued as universal, or to trivialize what is universal by identifying it with any local application. The world is their home, humankind have become their kind."[10]

FAMILY TRADITIONS: A CASE STUDY

Eduardo was failing two subjects in his senior year in high school. He knew he would not graduate unless things turned around drastically, but he didn't know what to do about it.

James had always admired Eduardo's basketball skills, but he began to notice a declining performance on the court. Being a peer counselor, James was able to ask Eduardo in a sensitive way if there was anything wrong. At first Eduardo was hesitant to say much, but James's caring manner helped him to open up.

Eduardo told James that he wouldn't be able to play basketball much longer since his grades had dropped recently. He expressed his disappointment about not having enough time for studies because of family obligations, including helping his father in the family business and looking after his younger brother. He was particularly worried about jeopardizing his high school graduation, since he would be the first one in his family to get a diploma. However, Eduardo felt his first commitment was to his family and seemed willing to sacrifice his grades if necessary.

James initially attempted to provide support and understanding to Eduardo. He reassured Eduardo that he wouldn't be a failure if he joined his father's business on a full-time basis and did not finish high school. Eduardo, however, responded somewhat negatively to James's approach. This puzzled James because he felt he was trying to be culturally sensitive. He remembered the importance of family commitments in Hispanic culture. James knew he needed further input from Mr. Muñoz, his peer counseling supervisor.

He had a long talk with him about how to better help Eduardo, realizing that he may have stereotyped Eduardo. Mr. Muñoz pointed out that he needed to explore more fully Eduardo's true feelings about academic achievement, suspecting that Eduardo really wanted to graduate from high school.

James followed Mr. Muñoz's suggestion in his next meeting with Eduardo. He was somewhat taken aback, but pleasantly surprised, by Eduardo's strong response. "I'm glad you asked me about my true feelings concerning graduation," Eduardo said. "Yes—I definitely want to graduate from high school and be the first person from my family to do so." He continued emphatically, "Of course I care about my family! But someone has to break the stereotype . . . this thing about Hispanics not wanting to do well academically is for the birds! I want to do well academically and I know I have the brains for it!"

With James's support and help, Eduardo did graduate that

year. James learned a valuable lesson in effective cross-cultural counseling: Beware of stereotyping and seek input from appropriate sources.

SECTION THREE:

The Basic Peer Counseling Training Course

SETTING THE STAGE

The preparation is complete. The exciting time of starting the training is at hand. Now what do you do? First you need to review your plans and make certain everything is in place. Your checklist needs to contain the following:

1. **Number of classes.** The number of classes will depend on how many hours you spend in each meeting. We suggest a total of forty-five to sixty hours of training. Sometimes this is broken down into two hours once a week, four hours on Saturday mornings, or even a retreat that will include sixteen hours of training in one weekend and then weekly meetings thereafter. The way your sessions are scheduled will depend on your needs and time commitments.

2. **Days and times.** Before the first class begins, the time schedule for the entire training should be completed. In fact, it is a good idea to give a copy of the schedule to each trainee at the first class meeting. Days and times should be marked clearly. A brief discussion and question period will give the trainees an opportunity to clarify any misunderstandings of dates or times.

3. **Location.** Will it be possible to meet at the same location each time, or will there be a need to move from time to time because of room scheduling conflicts? If the latter is necessary, then the location of the meetings should be placed by the date on the schedule the trainee receives. The location of all meetings should be scheduled on the church or parachurch organization's calendar before the first class begins.

4. **Content of the basic training course.** The basic training will consist of the following units:

Unit 1—The Bible and Peer Counseling
Unit 2—Meeting a Stranger and Developing Social Ease
Unit 3—Developing Active Listening Skills
Unit 4—Sending Effective Messages
Unit 5—Developing Self-Awareness and Building Self-Esteem
Unit 6—Developing Helping Skills
Unit 7—Problem Solving and Decision Making
Unit 8—Cross-Cultural Counseling
Unit 9—Starting and Ending a Helping Relationship
Unit 10—Referrals and Resources

Because you won't spend an equal amount of time on each unit, it is not possible to predict exactly how the forty-five to sixty hours of class time will be structured. There are, however, minimal amounts needed for each of the units of training. The time must be left flexible so you can use it effectively according to your needs, influenced largely by your class size. If your class has fifteen trainees in the fall, for instance, but in the spring the number in the new class has increased to thirty, the amount of time necessary for each class to develop active listening skills in Unit 3 will increase from eight hours to twelve hours, pushing the total number of hours of training from, say, fifty-six to sixty.

Although no rigid schedule exists, we have learned a few things from previous experiences that may serve as guidelines for you.

• In Unit 2 (Meeting a Stranger and Developing Social Ease), give the class ample time for everyone to get to know each other well before you move on to Unit 3. Learning and practicing how to meet a stranger will result in the class practicing with each other and getting to know everyone in the class well. Allow as much time as needed for this unit because this is when the class bonds together.

• More hours will be spent on Unit 3 (Developing Active Listening Skills) than any other unit. Active listening is the basis for most peer counseling activities, and the trainees must be prepared in this skill before moving on to the next unit. Each mem-

84

ber needs the opportunity to actively participate in class exercises. Although this may seem time-consuming to some leaders, it is absolutely necessary for the development of this skill.

• Unit 10 (Referrals and Resources) may take less time than some of the other units. However, you may choose to have various speakers from your church, parachurch organization, and community agencies visit the class at this time. This will result, of course, in increased course time.

• You may feel uncomfortable about not having a time schedule all mapped out prior to the training itself. Remember, though, that no one knows exactly how long each unit is going to take because the trainees themselves may take more time than you have scheduled for the "I feel" sessions. A peer counseling teacher/leader must be flexible.

Many times I've had to put lesson plans aside because a trainee's needs came first. During one training session a trainee asked to speak to the class about a problem. What normally might have taken only a few minutes ended up taking the entire meeting time because the trainee disclosed her incestuous relationship with her father. She had tried to talk to her mother about it years previously, but her mother had not believed her. This was the first time since then she had told anyone. It was infinitely more important to listen to this desperate girl than to proceed with the scheduled lesson.

HOW UNITS ARE ORGANIZED

The lesson plans in the following units are all presented in the following way:

Unit title

Suggested minimum time needed to complete the unit

Opening (including *Scripture Reading, Prayer,* and *"I feel" Session*)

Lesson (*Goals, Objectives, Purpose,* and *Content*)

Group participation (*Exercises*)

Closure

GO FOR IT!

Because your kids will not necessarily perfect their counseling skills by the close of these training sessions, remind them that their new peer counseling skills—like any new skill—will improve with practice. They will continue to role-play and do similar exercises in the advanced peer counseling training sessions, which will be conducted after the basic training course is completed.

Like varsity athletes, those students who do the best job will be the ones who practice their skills the most.

THE BIBLE AND PEER COUNSELING

Suggested minimum time needed for this unit: 4 hours

OPENING

• Greet all trainees at the door as they arrive. Call each person by name and ask how they are doing. Have name tags ready, since this is the first meeting and trainees may not know one another.

• Read Galatians 6:2. *Carry each other's burdens, and in this way you will fulfill the law of Christ.*

• Open with a short prayer. Ask for the Lord's guidance and blessing on the peer counseling training program and on the trainees present.

• With everyone seated in a circle, explain to the class that each training session will begin with an "I feel" session, starting with Unit 2. Since Unit 1 is the first session, ask the trainees to introduce themselves (name, grade level, school, favorite activity) and state why they are taking the peer counseling training course. Hand out the time schedule for the entire basic peer counseling training course and allow for a brief discussion period to clarify dates and times.

• Explain the rules of the class:

  ☐ *Confidentiality must be kept.* Encourage trainees to share openly and freely about themselves. This builds trust, and young people will share if they are assured that what is said in the room is not repeated outside the class. Make certain that everyone understands exactly what confidentiality means. The trainees will not repeat anything to anyone, with the following exceptions:

  1. Child or elder abuse must be reported to the police or

87

the department of social services. In such a case, the trainee may want to report this first to the peer counseling leader and ask for assistance in further reporting.

2. Potential suicide must be reported to an adult (the peer counseling leader, parent, guardian, mental health professional, or law enforcement).

3. Danger or harm to others must be reported to an adult (the peer counseling leader, parent, guardian, mental health professional, or law enforcement).

Ask trainees to sign and turn in their peer counseling confidentiality contracts (see Chapter Five), as well as their parent consent letters (see Chapter Five).

☐ *There are no "put downs" in the class.* The class will be an accepting place where everyone feels comfortable.

☐ *Honesty is imperative.* No one plays roles; masks are removed.

☐ *The class will come up with one word,* such as *support*, to be used if someone is unable to hear the speaker because of another person talking. Anyone in the class may say the word, and the class knows to come to immediate attention.

☐ *Anyone may pass during a sharing session* if he or she does not wish to share. No questions will be asked as to why they are passing.

LESSON

GOALS

• To learn the importance of a peer counseling ministry.
• To learn what the Bible says about human nature.
• To learn what the Bible says about how to do effective peer counseling.

OBJECTIVES

• Trainees will become aware of a few major Bible passages or verses that emphasize the importance of peer counseling.

• Trainees will become aware of the five major points about human nature based on the Bible.

• Trainees will become aware of the thirteen major points about how to do effective peer counseling based on the Bible and research (see p. 92; copy and distribute this sheet to the trainees).

PURPOSE

• Trainees need to know how to explain to others why peer counseling is important and valid based on the Bible itself.

• Trainees need to know how to think about human nature and the basic needs of human beings based on the Bible. They will need to keep these in mind as they do peer counseling.

• Trainees need to know how to use the thirteen points as guidelines to do effective peer counseling in a Christian, Bible-based way.

CONTENT

Read the following Bible verses:

"My command is this: Love each other as I have loved you" (John 15:12).

And we urge you, brothers, warn those who are idle, encourage the timid, help the weak, be patient with everyone (1 Thess. 5:14).

What the Bible Says about Human Nature

• *The basic emotional and spiritual needs of human beings* include longings for secure relationship (or love) and significant impact (or meaning) in order to have an appropriate sense of self-worth or self-acceptance (not selfishness or self-centeredness). Such longings are ultimately longings for God himself (Ps. 42:1, 2) and they can be substantially met only in the context of a personal relationship with Jesus Christ as one's Lord and Savior (Rom. 8:31–39).

• *The basic problem of human beings has to do with sin* (Rom. 3:23; Rom. 6:23), but not all emotional suffering is due to personal sin, or even the sins of others. Sometimes it may be due to obedience to God's will for the sake of our own growth to become more like Jesus (see Matt. 26:36–39; Mark 14:32–36; Luke 22:40–44; and Heb. 4:15, which relates that Jesus suffered but did not sin).

• *The ultimate goal of human beings is to know and enjoy God,* growing into greater Christlikeness (Rom. 8:29).

• *Problem feelings (depression and anxiety, for example) are usually (but not always) due to problem behavior* and, more fundamentally, problem thinking (see Prov. 23:7; John 8:32; Rom. 12:1–2; Eph. 4:22–24; Phil. 4:8). However, problem thinking is not always at the root of all emotional problems. Biological factors like chemical imbalances in the brain may be the reason for certain severe emotional disorders (manic-depressive mood swings, for example) where psychiatric help should be sought. Furthermore, demonic forces may underlie other severe emotional and spiritual disturbances, in which case, pastors and church leaders should be consulted.

• *A holistic view of persons is essential,* including the physical, mental/emotional, social, and spiritual dimensions of human functioning (see Luke 2:52 and the example of Jesus growing in these four areas of life).

GROUP PARTICIPATION

EXERCISE 1

Ask the trainees to discuss and memorize John 15:12, Galatians 6:2, and 1 Thessalonians 5:14. If they need more time to memorize, encourage them to work on the verses at home during the following week. Emphasize the *biblical basis* of peer counseling as a ministry, not just as something worthwhile to do.

EXERCISE 2

Ask the trainees to discuss the five major points about human nature. Clarify for them any confusion or misunderstanding they may have (see Chapter Two for further details and explanations of these points).

EXERCISE 3

Ask the trainees to discuss the thirteen distinctives of biblical peer counseling. Clear up any confusion or misunderstanding. Use examples from Chapter Two if you want.

CLOSURE

• Reassure trainees that the large amount of information and Bible knowledge presented and discussed in each session, and particularly in these first sessions, will take some time and further training sessions to sink in. References to that material will be made repeatedly in future sessions.
• Give a brief promotional about the next session.
• Close in prayer.

Thirteen Distinctives of Effective Peer Counseling, Based on the Bible and Research

- **The Holy Spirit's ministry as Counselor or Comforter is crucial** (John 14:16, 17). Depend on him in prayer, for guidance, wisdom, and healing power.

- **The Bible is a basic guide to helping people with problems** (2 Tim. 3:16, 17). Use it wisely and appropriately when possible.

- **Prayer is a crucial part of effective biblical peer counseling** (James 5:16). Pray with and for the counselee when possible.

- **The ultimate goal of peer counseling is to help Christians become more like Jesus** (Rom. 8:29), or to grow spiritually, and to help non-Christians come closer to knowing Jesus as their own Lord and Savior, and therefore fulfill the Great Commission (Matt. 28:18–20).

- **The personal spiritual qualities of the peer counselor are important:** especially goodness or love, knowledge of the Bible (Rom. 15:14), wisdom (Col. 3:16), maturity (Gal. 6:12), and the spiritual gift of exhortation or encouragement (Rom. 12:8).

- **The counselee's attitudes, motivations, and desire for help are critical.** Those who are actively involved in their counseling do better than those who are withdrawn, defensive, or hostile.

- **The quality of the relationship between the peer counselor and the counselee is very important.** There should be good rapport and communication based on empathy (understanding), respect (caring), concreteness (being specific), genuineness (being real), confrontation (telling it like it is), and immediacy (what's really going on between the two of you). The Bible calls this "speaking the truth in love" (Eph. 4:15).

- **Effective peer counseling involves exploration, understanding, and action phases,** with a focus on changing problem thinking. Active listening and problem-solving skills are crucial (more about this in Units 3 and 7).

- **The style or approach in peer counseling should be flexible depending on the counselee and the problem** (1 Thess. 5:14).

- **The specific techniques or methods of counseling should be consistent with the Bible's teaching and values** (1 Thess. 5:21).

- **Cultural sensitivity and cross-cultural counseling skills are needed by the peer counselor** (see Unit 8).

- **Skills in outreach and prevention are also important**—for example, helping counselees to be connected to appropriate resources of community help and social support, including church and parachurch youth groups.

- **Awareness of their own limitations and knowing when and how to refer** are also important (see Unit 10) for Christian peer counselors.

MEETING A STRANGER AND DEVELOPING SOCIAL EASE

Suggested minimum time needed for this unit: 6 hours

OPENING

• Greet everyone at the door as they arrive. Call each person by name and do a quick check as to how that person is feeling ("Hello, how are you? Looking good!").

• If people do not yet know each other, have name tags ready.

• Read Romans 15:7. *Accept one another, then, just as Christ accepted you, in order to bring praise to God.*

• Open with a short prayer. Do not call on anyone to pray unless you have previously checked it out with him or her.

• Conduct the first "I feel" session. Each person will be given the opportunity to share any feelings he or she may be having: "I feel great because I got an A on a math test," "I feel lousy because I just found out my parents are getting a divorce," and so on. All others in the circle give the speaker their undivided attention. During the "I feel" session, others in the group may ask questions of the speaker, but answering those questions is optional. Each person will take his or her turn until everyone in the circle has had an opportunity to speak. If someone's turn comes up and he or she chooses not to speak, that person may say, "I pass." No questions or looks of disapproval are allowed. The "I feel" sessions may require varied amounts of time. If the class meets only once a week, it is important to have an "I feel" session each time. If the meetings are more frequent, the "I feel" session may be limited to once a week.

LESSON

GOAL

• To learn how to talk to strangers and feel at ease.

OBJECTIVE

• Trainees will become proficient in using the skill required to reach out to someone he or she does not know.

PURPOSE

Explain why it is important for peer counselors to know how to meet a stranger.

• Their counselees may be strangers to them.

• They need to know how to approach young people who are sitting alone at lunchtime, standing alone at a social gathering, sitting alone at church, or walking alone on campus.

Peer counselors often find their counselees by simply being observant. A loner often needs a friend to talk to, and the peer counselor may fill that need.

CONTENT

The "Steps in Meeting a Stranger" that are detailed on p. 96 will help your trainees gain confidence with strangers. Make copies for all students.

GROUP PARTICIPATION

EXERCISE 1

Divide the class into pairs; trainees should pair up with someone they do not know, or whom they know little about. Give them ten minutes to introduce themselves and to get to know their partners. Have everyone return to their chairs. Place two chairs in the center of the circle. Invite each couple, one after another, to come to the middle of the circle, introduce their partner and tell the class about him or her. Continue this exercise until all members of the class have had the opportunity to introduce their partners. Not only have the trainees practiced their skill, but they have also enabled each member of the class to get to know everyone a little bit better.

EXERCISE 2

Divide the class up according to birthday months or seasons of the year (winter, spring, summer, fall) that trainees were born in. Instruct the groups to each talk among themselves about other things they have in common. Have the groups return to the circle and share what they have learned about each other. This exercise may also be done using regions of the country people were born in, favorite colors, or anticipated careers.

EXERCISE 3

Have one trainee assume the role of the peer counselor and another the role of the stranger as the two meet for the first time. (Trainees may want to review the ten steps of meeting a stranger.) Allow the trainees to role-play before the group for five minutes. After they have finished, ask the class for positive input about what they saw and heard. This exercise may be repeated, using different trainees each time.

EXERCISE 4

Brainstorm times in the Bible when Jesus met a stranger (the woman at the well in John 4, for example). List characteristics of Jesus when he talked to the strangers. Which of these characteristics would the class most like to have as peer counselors (such as listening attentively)?

CLOSURE

• Review the session by asking the trainees to state one new thing they have each learned.
• Give a brief promotional about the next lesson.
• Close in prayer.

Steps in Meeting a Stranger

1. Introduce yourself to the stranger. If the stranger does not reciprocate with a name, you may request it.

2. Initiate conversation by talking about the present surroundings (decorations at a party or score at a basketball game) or common interests between you (both of you may enjoy the music being played).

3. You'll learn more about the stranger if you listen attentively and observe body language.

4. Encourage the stranger to talk about himself or herself. Observe any unusual jewelry or clothing and ask about it. Strangers will probably feel comfortable talking about what they know best. A girl may explain that the necklace she is wearing belonged to her grandmother, or a boy may talk freely about the basketball shirt he is wearing and where he purchased it.

5. Be careful not to ask questions of a personal or intrusive nature. If the stranger feels that you're prying into his or her privacy, the conversation may terminate quickly.

6. Do not ask questions that require a yes or no answer. This puts you in the position of having to carry the conversation. Ask open-ended questions that usually begin with "How" or "What."

7. Let the stranger know that you're sincere in your interest. Insincerity can be spotted a mile away. A stranger deserves sincerity and respect.

8. Proper closure to the conversation is important. You may set up another meeting or exchange phone numbers with the new friend.

9. If the stranger is new to the school, church, or youth organization, introduce him or her to other people.

10. If the stranger has revealed certain interests, you may want to connect him or her to a club on campus or a sports team at the church or organization, if it is appropriate.

DEVELOPING ACTIVE LISTENING SKILLS

Suggested minimum time needed for this unit: 8 hours

OPENING

- This is one of the most important units in the training. Allow each student time to practice developing his or her skill; do not rush them.
- Read Proverbs 18:13. *He who answers before listening—that is his folly and his shame.*
- Open with prayer.
- Lead an "I feel" session.

LESSON

GOALS

- To teach the skill of active listening.
- To give the peer counselors the opportunity to practice this skill by role-playing with each other.

OBJECTIVE

- Trainees will learn the art of active listening by participating in class activities.

PURPOSE

- Explain to the class that active listening is important because it enables the peer counselor to help the *counselee* to solve his or her own problems.
- Remind the students that listening involves more than merely paying attention to what someone is saying. Just having open ears does not meet the requirements for being a good listener.
- Explain to the class that they will need to know how to listen and how to respond in a manner that will allow speakers to be

comfortable in talking to them and open with their feelings.

CONTENT

Listening has been described as a lost art in our society today. Everyone is so busy running from project to project that it seems only a few people take time to sit down and really listen to someone else. Yet, the importance of listening has never been denied. If a person is listened to, he or she feels valued. The person's confidence is strengthened; his or her self-esteem raised. By listening to a person, you are saying to him or her, "You are important to me. I am taking my valuable time to listen to you. You have my love and my acceptance."

Norman Wakefield stated, "Listening says, 'I want to understand you. I want to know you.' It is one of the most basic ways to convey a sense of respect, to treat another person with dignity. Through this act we affirm to another person that God is willing to listen, that he eagerly waits for his troubled child to come to him and discover the compassion and deep concern of his loving Father."[1]

Sometimes a person has an emotional need to talk as an outlet for stored-up thoughts about good news or problems. This person does not want to be challenged, judged, advised, debated, interrupted, or sidetracked into a maze of detail. He or she is saying, "Please just listen to me. I need to share my thoughts and feelings. I need to understand myself. For that I need your patience and tolerance, for I may not be logical, clear, or correct. But wait until I've expressed myself completely before you point this out to me."

In the peer counseling class, the students must understand the importance of good listening, and they must work diligently until they have acquired the skill and can use it naturally. As in any skill, success comes with practice.

GROUP PARTICIPATION

EXERCISE 1

Make certain the group knows the difference between ordinary listening (as one would listen to his or her best friend) and active listening, which involves the characteristics listed on the hand-out sheet, "The Skill of Active Listening" (see p. 102). Explain that ordinary listening involves two people sharing thoughts, ideas, feelings with one another. Both people spend time talking back and forth. Active listening involves one person talking and one person listening. Instead of each person sharing, as in ordinary listening, only one person shares in active listening. Discuss the reason for this: When the second person begins to share, the focus is taken away from the original speaker and his or her problem.

Discuss each characteristic of active listening and ask for feelings and questions about each one.

EXERCISE 2

One of the best ways to develop the skill of active listening is to role-play. One person assumes the role of the peer counselor and the other one acts as the counselee. Ask the counselee to share a real problem if possible. This not only gives students opportunities to share their problems, but it also makes the role-playing more meaningful and realistic. Explain that the problem may be minor or major, according to the degree of openness with which the counselee feels comfortable.

Instruct the class to listen for and observe the characteristics of active listening being demonstrated. After the role-playing is complete, ask the students to respond to the question: *"According to our discussion about the characteristics of active listening, what things did you observe that were done well in the role-playing situation?"* After the class has had sufficient time for discussion, then ask, *"What things would you have done differently if you'd been doing the role-playing?"* Never ask trainees, "What did he/she do wrong?" This might make the student hesitate to volunteer for role-playing in the future for fear of doing something wrong. Allow time for discussion of this second question.

EXERCISE 3

The group leader reads the following statements and asks the class for appropriate reflective listening responses.

A. "I don't know what I'm going to do. My parents are getting a divorce and mom wants me to live with her and dad wants me to live with him."

An appropriate response: "You sound confused as to what your decision should be."

B. "I don't want to face my family because I told them I'd be the senior class president next year. Today I lost by only two votes."

An appropriate response: "Losing the election has caused you to feel embarrassed, especially after the premature announcement to your family."

C. "Today has been the worst day of the year! My car wouldn't start, so I had to walk to school. I was late getting here, and I had to go to the attendance office for a tardy slip. Then when I got to class, I realized I'd left my term paper at home, and I was going to lose ten points off the grade for not turning it in at the end of the period."

An appropriate response: "You sound upset because of the many things that went wrong today."

D. "It is my own fault I didn't get the job. Several days ago, Mom told me to pick up an application, but I procrastinated. When I finally got around to it, the position was already filled."

An appropriate response: "It sounds like you feel a little regretful and guilty because you weren't more prompt in following your mom's suggestion."

E. "I've just found out my best friend asked my girlfriend to go to the basketball game with him. I can't believe he'd do such a thing."

An appropriate response: "You're shocked at what your best friend did to you."

F. "My parents told me I could have my car back if I brought up my grades, but now they've changed their minds after I've done what they wanted."

An appropriate response: "You sound angry because your parents didn't do what they told you they'd do."

G. "I never believed I'd get the lead in the play. When my name was called, I jumped up and ran onto the stage."

An appropriate response: "You sound very excited and happy about getting the part."

EXERCISE 4

Divide the class into groups of threes. One trainee role-plays a peer counselor, while another role-plays a counselee, with a real-life problem if possible. The focus is on active listening. The third trainee observes the role-play for ten minutes or so, then provides feedback and joins a discussion with the two trainees playing the roles. The role-playing trainees then switch roles and do a second role-play.

CLOSURE

• Ask the students to practice their active listening skills with a family member during the next week. Suggest to them that they record their conversation on audiotape, if possible. Reviewing the tape enables trainees to evaluate their strengths and weaknesses.

• Review the reason why active listening is so important. Stress the need for continued practice in developing the skill.

• Close in prayer.

The Skill of Active Listening*

- How to listen actively:

  ☐ Reflect the counselee's most important thoughts and feelings by restating what you think you have heard.

  ☐ Convey understanding and acceptance by nonverbal behavior. Notice what messages you are sending by your posture, tone of voice, eye contact, facial expressionas, and gestures.

  ☐ Try to understand what the person is saying (content) and how he or she feels by putting yourself in the other's place.

  ☐ Do not interrupt the counselee or bring up similar feelings or problems from your own experiences.

  ☐ Be attentive and don't daydream. Keep your thoughts from wandering and focus them on the speaker.

  ☐ Do not be an advice giver. If specific directions or instructions *are* necessary, make sure the advice is not premature or excessive.

  ☐ Do not argue mentally with yourself ("self-talk").

  ☐ Do not make hasty judgments and thus antagonize the speaker.

  ☐ Have a desire to listen. It may be true that there are no uninteresting people—only disinterested listeners.

  ☐ React appropriately by applauding with nods, smiles, comments, and encouragements.

  ☐ Listen for camouflaged feelings and ask yourself what feelings you think you are hearing. Often feelings are hiding behind words.

  ☐ Avoid changing the subject. If you do get off track, refocus on the actual issue.

  ☐ Develop the attitude that listening is enjoyable and personally rewarding.

- Active listening involves reflecting to the speaker both his or her *content* (what the speaker is saying) as well as *feelings* (how the speaker seems to feel about what he or she is saying).

- Active listening shows that you empathize with your counselee.

*Adapted from Joan Sturkie, *Enjoy Your Kids: Enjoy Your Work* (Waco, Tex.: Word, 1991), 113.

SENDING EFFECTIVE MESSAGES

Suggested minimum time needed for this unit: 4 hours

OPENING

• Read James 1:19, 26. *My dear brothers, take note of this: Everyone should be quick to listen, slow to speak and slow to become angry. . . . If anyone considers himself religious and yet does not keep a tight rein on his tongue, he deceives himself and his religion is worthless.*
• Open with prayer.
• Lead an "I feel" session.

LESSON

GOALS

• To make students aware of the messages they are sending.
• To teach them a more effective way of communicating these messages.

OBJECTIVE

• Trainees will learn to send effective messages by participating in the class exercises.

PURPOSE

• The class needs to know that what we say is sometimes meant differently than what listeners hear.
• A breakdown in communication, and sometimes a fracture in a relationship, may be caused by messages being received with a different meaning than was intended. Peer counselors need to know what effective messages are and be skilled in how to send them.

CONTENT

Effective messages are those that are most likely to be heard and understood by the person who receives them. Sending effective messages is a skill, and there are certain guidelines to assist in learning it (see p. 106).

GROUP PARTICIPATION

EXERCISE 1

Photocopy p. 107 and cut on the dotted lines. Divide the students into three groups. Give each trainee in the first group a copy of "Group One," each trainee in the second group a copy of "Group Two," and so on. Ask them to work together as a group and to be prepared to present their section's information to the entire class.

After the groups have worked separately, ask them to come together and present their lesson.

EXERCISE 2

Divide the group into threes. Ask one person to be the *listener*, one the *speaker*, and the other the *observer*. The listener and the speaker role-play a situation. The observer watches the body language and listens for congruent and noncongruent messages and "I" statements. After the session is completed, the observer tells what he or she has observed. The three students then rotate positions until each one has had an opportunity to be an observer.

EXERCISE 3

Divide the group into two teams. Ask one team to present five statements that are *not* "I" statements; the other team to restate the comment using an "I" statement.

Example:
Team One: "You disappoint me with your lack of commitment."
Team Two: "I'm feeling confused and disappointed because I do not understand your apparent lack of commitment."

After fifteen minutes reverse the duties of each team.

CLOSURE

• Ask the students to observe conversations during the next week and to listen for "I" statements.

• Review the importance of body language, sending congruent messages, and "I" statements.

• Close in prayer.

Sending Effective Messages

- Personal feelings are best expressed by using "I" statements. Use your own feelings about the person who will receive the message. For example, you should say, "I am angry with you because—" instead of "You make me angry when you—." When you place blame on the receiver by saying, "You make me angry . . . " a barrier immediately goes up on the receiver's side, and good communication is impossible.

- Your verbal and nonverbal messages must be congruent. In other words, body language should match spoken words. If you state that you are not angry, but your face is red and your words are curt, you are sending an noncongruent message. The receiver may be confused because your body language and your words are saying two different things. He or she may not know whether to listen to your verbal or your nonverbal message. Congruent messages are those that do not confuse the receiver. You give a congruent message when you state that you are happy and have a smile on your face. The receiver has no doubt as to how the person is feeling.

- Convey explicit expectations in your messages as to what you want the other person to change. Otherwise, the receiver of the message may perpetuate his or her personal dilemma, believing he or she is powerless to resolve the situation.

- You must take responsibility for—"own"— your own feelings and actions. You are in charge of your own feelings. Although you sometimes cannot control *how* you feel, you do have responsibility for how you *express* your feelings.

- You must communicate care for and acceptance of the receiver's feelings and reactions to your message. Use reflective listening statements, such as "I hear you saying you are lonely."

Exercises for Sending Effective Messages

Group One

Explain to your fellow trainees what "I" messages are: Assuming ownership for the feeling and expressing it by using the word "I."

- Example of a student using an "I" message when talking to a teacher: "I feel confused and angry because of my C in biology." By using the word *I*, the speaker is taking ownership for his or her own feelings, and the receiver of the message is more responsive to helping solve the problem.

- Example of a student not using an "I" message when talking to a teacher: "You make me so angry because you gave me a C in biology." By using the word *you*, the receiver of the message immediately puts barriers up and is not open to what else may be said. The receiver may feel threatened by the attack and become angry.

Group Two

Explain to the group the difference between a congruent and a noncongruent message.

- Example: Smiling speaker says, "I'm feeling so sad today." This is a noncongruent message because the body language and the spoken words do not match. The receiver does not know whether to believe the words or the body language. Noncongruent messages confuse listeners.

- Example: Smiling speaker says, "I'm feeling great today." This is a congruent message. Words and body language match.

Group Three

Talk to the whole group about the importance of body language and what messages are sent by nonverbal communication.
- Discuss the importance of not crossing the arms, hands, legs, or feet when participating as an active listener. Crossed positions may convey to the speaker that we are "closed" to hearing them.
- Other body language to note is the importance of an appropriate nod or smile and good eye contact. The listener may want to lean his or her body slightly toward the speaker.

DEVELOPING SELF-AWARENESS AND BUILDING SELF-ESTEEM

Suggested minimum time needed for this unit: 4 hours

OPENING

- Read Philippians 4:13. *I can do everything through him who gives me strength.*
- Open with prayer.
- Lead an "I feel" session.

LESSON

GOALS

- To allow the students to become more aware of self.
- To place value and respect on oneself as God has instructed us to do as his children.

OBJECTIVE

- Trainees will participate in exercises that will make them more aware of themselves in the light of Christ's love.

PURPOSE

- Peer counselors will come into contact with peers who have very low self-esteem. In order to help others help themselves, peer counselors need to know the value of a healthy self-esteem.
- A healthy self-esteem does not refer to being filled with vanity and pride, but is instead a deeper, more meaningful awareness of knowing God loves us. With his help we can accomplish many things, be successful, and live productive lives.

CONTENT

Self-esteem is a feeling of personal self-worth and therefore peers who have high self-esteem feel good about themselves. Those with low self-esteem usually find life to be unfulfilling. Peer counselors will want to help their counselees develop confidence and courage, so they will be prepared to face their problems.

Various problems brought to peer counselors by young people often have a common root—poor self-esteem. A peer counselor in the training sessions may also have a very poor self-image. I remember a young man in a peer counseling class saying, "When I first entered this class I felt like garbage, but now after a semester I feel like a human being." We often do not realize how really low some young people are feeling, low enough to feel like garbage.

In *The One Minute Manager*, author Kenneth Blanchard states, "People who feel good about themselves produce good results."[1] For peer counselors to produce good results, they must feel good about themselves.

Healthy self-esteem gives a person the ability to respond to the opportunities of life in an active and positive way. The peer counselor can make a difference in a counselee's life by helping that person realize how important self-esteem really is.

From a Christian perspective, a person's self-esteem or sense of personal self-worth is based on God's love for him or her, manifested in a meaningful and loving, personal relationship with the Lord Jesus Christ—who ultimately is the only one who can save us from our sins and make us whole persons again. The Christian peer counselor will help a Christian counselee to grow in the knowledge and experience of God's love and God's acceptance of him or her—what David Seamands has termed "healing grace" (which is also the title of one of his books).[2]

In 1990, the California Department of Education released the results of a three-year study on self-esteem, *Toward a State of Esteem: The Final Report of the California Task Force to Promote Self-Esteem and Personal and Social Responsibility*.[3] This report correlates the boosting of self-esteem with the reduction of crime, drug use, and other antisocial activities. It suggests ways for individuals to foster a healthier self-esteem in themselves.

Many of the points on p. 113 are incorporated into the basic peer counseling training. Students are trained to listen, accept and respect themselves and others, be honest, have values, be a spiritual person, be accountable, express feelings, and serve humanity. In learning how to be a peer counselor, the trainee is doing the very things that *Toward a State of Esteem* suggests people should do in order to raise their own self-esteem. No wonder peer counselors talk about feeling better about themselves.

GROUP PARTICIPATION

EXERCISE 1

Pass out a 5 x 7 note card to all students in the class. Instruct each student to place his or her name on the top right corner of the card and pass the card to the person sitting on the right. Instruct the students to write one positive comment on the card that describes the person whose name appears at the top. The comment must be an honest feeling. If a student chooses not to write, he or she may pass the card to the next person. Then pick up the cards after everyone has written a comment *but before the card reaches its owner.* Shuffle the cards and then pass them out again to someone different from the name written at the top. Taking turns, each person then reads the comments on the card he or she is holding, and the class tries to guess to whom the card belongs. After the positive comments are correctly matched with a student, give the card to that student. Encourage the students to keep their cards and read them in the future when they want to remember how positive their peers feel about them.

EXERCISE 2

A medium-sized teddy bear will be needed for this exercise. While you hold the teddy bear, give someone in the circle a positive comment—though without saying the name of the person until the end of the comment. At that time hand the teddy bear to the complimented person, perhaps with a hug. That person then gives positive comments about another person, and the teddy bear is passed on to that person. The teddy bear continues to go from one person to another until everyone in the room receives it. It's okay for students to get the teddy bear more than once. Instruct the students that everything that is said must be honest, and that if anyone wishes to pass, he or she may.

CLOSURE

• Ask the trainees to write an affirmation on each of four medium-sized Post-it note stickers. For example: "I am capable and willing" or "I am a good listener" or "I have a nice smile." These affirmations may be Scripture verses (perhaps even the one read at the beginning of class). Instruct the trainees to place these stickers where they will see them daily (on their bedroom door or bathroom mirror, for example).

• Close in prayer.

Nurturing Your Self-Esteem*

- **Accept and appreciate yourself.** Each person is a unique individual and needs to celebrate his or her special race, ethnicity, culture, gender, abilities, and creativity.

- **Forgive yourself and others.** To forgive is to stop resenting. When we let go of resentment toward ourselves and others, we live happier lives.

- **Express your feelings.** To grow as individuals we need to increase our capacity to express our true feelings in a way that is not harmful to ourselves or others.

- **Appreciate your spiritual being.** Awareness of our spiritual dimension helps us to see ourselves as persons of value and worth.

- **Trust yourself and others.** Trusting ourselves, our judgment, and our competence inspires and educates others to trust themselves. Trusting others communicates that they are trustworthy.

- **Set realistic expectations.** Goals must be appropriate and attainable. Expecting too little of ourselves does not dignify our human spirit; expecting too much can invite failure.

- **Take risks.** It is usually easier and more comfortable to live with a problem than it is to take steps to solve it. We grow by taking risks and inviting change.

- **Appreciate your body and mind.** Paying attention to the healthy development of the body and the mind helps us strengthen our capacity to resist distress, illness, and addictions. Making a conscious decision to understand, maintain, and develop our physical soundness and mental faculties is essential to physical and mental health, self-esteem, and responsible behavior.

- **Take responsibility for your own decisions and actions.** Accepting responsibility means not blaming other people or circumstances if our choices prove to be painful or in error.

- **Be a person of integrity.** Being honest in our dealings with other people is essential to valuing ourselves.

- **Understand and affirm your values.** Practicing our basic values helps us to grow and become our unique selves.

- **Serve humanity.** Persons with healthy self-esteem choose to serve others out of their sense of personal fullness and their joy of being alive. In the process of serving, we deepen and reinforce our own self-esteem.

*Toward a State of Esteem: The Final Report of the California Task Force to Promote Self-Esteem and Personal and Social Responsibility (Sacramento, Calif.: Bureau of Publications, California Department of Education, 1990).

DEVELOPING HELPING SKILLS

Suggested minimum time needed for this unit: 4 hours

OPENING

- Read 1 Thessalonians 5:14. *And we urge you, brothers, warn those who are idle, encourage the timid, help the weak, be patient with everyone.*
- Open with prayer.
- Lead an "I feel" session.

LESSON

GOALS

- To teach the responsibilities of a helper.
- To raise awareness of the difference between acceptance and agreement.
- To teach the students to ask questions effectively.

OBJECTIVES

- Trainees will learn what it means to be a helper.
- Trainees will become aware of the difference between acceptance and agreement.
- Trainees will learn how to ask questions effectively.

PURPOSE

- Students need to know how to help another person. They are trained to allow the counselee to make his or her own decisions.
- Peer counselors do not "rescue."

CONTENT

Peer counselors do not solve counselee's problems. Rather, they help the counselee to solve his or her own problems (see p. 120).

Rescuing

"Rescuing" takes place when the peer counselor takes the consequences of the counselee's action upon himself or herself and "saves" the counselee from being responsible for his or her own actions. For example, Brian drinks too much at parties on the weekend, and he asks Mack, his peer counselor, if he can stay at his house overnight. Mack has been counseling Brian for several weeks, and he knows Brian has problems at home. Not wanting to tell Brian no because of his fear that Brian will get into more trouble with his mom if he goes home intoxicated, Mack tells Brian he may stay overnight at his house. After several weeks of this type of behavior being repeated over and over, Mack realizes that he is rescuing Brian. Instead of helping Brian, Mack is contributing to Brian's behavior of continuing to repeat the weekend pattern.

Acceptance or Agreement

Peer counselors often ask what they are to do if they do not agree with a decision the counselee is making. Explain to the student that there is a difference between acceptance and agreement. They may accept the counselee's decision even if it isn't what the peer counselor would choose to do. Jessalyn, for example, decided to postpone going to college and chose to work a year instead so she could have a new car. Cheryl, her peer counselor, would not have made the same decision for herself, but realized the choice was Jessalyn's. This is *acceptance*, as opposed to *agreement*, which happens when the counselee makes a decision that is the same or very similar to a decision the peer counselor would make.

There does not need to be agreement between the peer counselor and the counselee at all times. Sometimes there may only be acceptance. However, a peer counselor is never asked to go against his or her own value system. Jane asked Susan, a peer counselor, to counsel her about getting an abortion. Susan does not believe in abortion, and she tells Jane that she will be glad to listen; however, because of her position on abortion, she cannot support Jane's decision.

Asking Questions

Peer counselors spend a lot of time listening to counselees—and in order to gather information, counselors need to ask questions. Three kinds of questions are commonly asked.

• **Closed questions** ask for specific information: "Did you keep your doctor's appointment?" Closed questions usually begin with "Is . . . ?" "Did . . . ?" or "Have . . . ?" and are usually answered with a yes or no. Peer counselors should try to stay away from closed questions, especially at the beginning of the counseling relationship.

• **Open-ended questions** encourage conversation because feelings are allowed to be discussed. The most effective questions usually begin with "How . . . ?" or "What . . . ?"

• **"Why . . . ?" questions** should be used infrequently, because they often put the receiver on the defensive. Sometimes "Why . . . ?" questions make people feel they must explain or justify what has happened.

GROUP PARTICIPATION

EXERCISE 1

Ask for two volunteers to move their chairs to the center of a circle. One assumes the role of the peer counselor and the other the counselee. Ask the counselee to share an actual problem. (Actual problems are more realistic for the others in class; also the trainee-counselee may be helped by talking about it. But remember: the trainee *can* "pass.") Ask the class to listen for ways the counselor helps the counselee solve his or her own problem. After the role-playing is over, ask for a discussion of whether the goal was accomplished.

EXERCISE 2

Ask the students to think of issues about which they might disagree with a counselee. Ask for one student to write everyone's comments on a blackboard. Suggestions may include taking drugs, cheating on tests, having an abortion, obeying (or disobeying) parents, dropping out of school, running away from home.

After the list is complete, ask trainees to discuss which items on the board they could have *acceptance* with, and which ones they could have *agreement* with. Explain to the students that sometimes they must refer the student to another counselor because they have neither acceptance nor agreement with this counselee.

EXERCISE 3

Divide the group into threes. In a role-playing situation, ask one student to be a peer counselor, one the counselee, and the third an observer. Ask the observer to listen for open, closed, or "Why . . . ?" questions—then discuss them with the counselor and counselee after the role-playing is over. Rotate positions of the students and continue role-playing.

EXERCISE 4

Ask the students to divide into pairs and role-play the part of the counselor and the counselee. Assign to each group various problems. For example, one student may play the role of a peer counselor who has the tendency to rescue. Other roles to play might include the following:
• An advice giver or problem solver.
• A counselor who gets over-involved emotionally.
• A counselor who feels guilty or angry if the problem is not being solved.

A variation of this activity could include a third person—an observer—who offers input after the role-playing is completed.

After everyone has completed the role-play in small groups, choose three or four groups to reenact their role-playing situation before the entire class.

CLOSURE

• Review the session and ask for any questions or clarifications.
• Ask the students to listen for open and closed questions in their conversations outside of peer counseling class.
• Close in prayer.

Why Counselors Shouldn't Solve Counselees' Problems

- What you tell a counselee to do may have worked for you, but that doesn't mean it will work for the counselee. Every person is unique, and different solutions work for different people.

- If your solution doesn't work for the counselee, he or she may not return for your continued help. After all, the counselee may think, "What my counselor said to do didn't work." Thus, you probably have lost your credibility with the counselee.

- If counselees have their decisions made for them by someone else, or are always given solutions, they will not learn to make decisions. Counselees with this habit will always turn to someone to make the decision for them. If they are in a situation where help is not available, they do not know what to do.

PROBLEM SOLVING AND DECISION MAKING

Suggested minimum time needed for this unit: 4 hours

OPENING

- Read Proverbs 3:5–6. *Trust in the Lord with all your heart and lean not on your own understanding; in all your ways acknowledge him and he will make your paths straight.*
- Open with prayer.
- Lead an "I feel" session.

LESSON

GOAL

- To teach students ways of solving problems and making decisions.

OBJECTIVE

- Trainees will become familiar with problem solving and will learn the steps in a decision-making model.

PURPOSE

Many times a teenager will approach a peer counselor to seek help in problem solving or decision making. Often the counselee is not aware of the available options. Counselors need to know how to assist their counselees in solving their conflicts and in making them aware of a decision-making process.

CONTENT

Conflict is a disagreement, dispute, or quarrel of any duration. Conflicts are inevitable in life because of differences that polarize, if not alienate, people. Peer counselors should develop skills

121

to recognize and deal with conflict.

Young people experience a variety of conflicts, whether internal (centering around the person's struggle with himself or herself) or external (involving the person's relationship with one or more people). Conflicts may be conscious or unconscious. A teenager may experience turmoil or a sense of unrest and may not recognize that a state of conflict exists.

Throughout much of humankind's history, conflict has been usually dealt with in one of two ways: fight or flight. Fortunately, conflicts can be resolved by identifying the problem, listening to complaints, seeking alternatives, gathering information, planning action, and reviewing the outcome.

Decisions are made based on tradition, authority, values, or impulse. A family's annual vacation to Colorado each year is probably the result of a decision based on tradition. When a teenager decides to go to traffic school rather than pay a traffic ticket, that decision is based on authority. When a high school girl decides to not look at a stolen copy of a upcoming math test being passed around her class, her decision is based on her values. When a high school senior, out on a date, buys an expensive bracelet for his girlfriend after she has admired it in a jewelry store window, that decision is probably based on impulse.

Peer counselors are called upon frequently when a counselee has a difficult decision to make. Many young people who seek out a peer counselor for help have no idea how to go about making a good decision. It is imperative that the peer counselors be trained in this skill.

GROUP PARTICIPATION

EXERCISE 1

Role-playing is an especially effective way for trainees to learn decision-making skills. Ask one student and another peer to move their chairs to center circle and role-play, using the decision-making model found on p. 124. The counselee's problem should be a real one ("I can't decide what college to go to"), so that the counselor can do realistic follow-up.

EXERCISE 2

Divide the class into pairs. Instruct them to role-play a peer counselor and a counselee who proceed through the decision-making steps concerning a dilemma that the counselee raises. Rotate the roles of peer counselor and counselee.

EXERCISE 3

Ask the class to discuss ways in which they try to discern what God's will is for them in specific areas of their lives. During the discussion, you may want to draw particular attention to prayer, guidance from the Bible, seeking godly counsel from spiritually mature mentors, direction from the Holy Spirit, and circumstantial leading (the opening and closing of opportunities, for example).

CLOSURE

• Review the decision-making model. Encourage the students to refer to the steps in this model until they become very familiar with the process.
• Close in prayer.

How to Help Counselees Solve Problems and Make Wise Decisions*

- **Clarify feelings.** Help your counselee sort out what his or her true feelings really are. Use active listening skills to accomplish this. List several of these feelings to help the counselee identify which ones fit the situation.

- **Gather information.** Learn as much as you can about the details surrounding the decision.

- **Define the problem.** Ask the counselee what he or she thinks the problem is. The *primary* problem may not be the first one he or she presents to you when the counseling begins.

- **Identify the decision.** What does the counselee want to change? Use open-ended, feeling-level questions to find out what needs to be changed and where the counselee wants to end up after the decision is made.

- **Brainstorm alternatives.** Ask the counselee what choices he or she has. You can contribute to this list and you may want to write alternatives down so the counselee can see them all at one time.

- **Evaluate the alternatives.** After each alternative has been discussed, mentioning both the pros and the cons, ask the counselee to prioritize them or rate their importance.

- **Predict consequences.** What will be the result of the decision? Carefully discuss each outcome of every decision being considered.

- **Clarify values.** Discuss the decision in relation to the counselee's values. If the counselee feels the decision conflicts with his or her values, brainstorm other alternatives.

- **Support the decision.** If the counselee is ready to make a decision, support it (unless the decision violates biblical values—in which case, you may need to gently confront your counselee, or perhaps agree to disagree—but all with caring acceptance of the counselee as a person). If more time is needed to gather further information, establish another time to meet.

- **Make an action plan.** Help the counselee decide what must be first, second, third, fourth, and fifth in order to carry out the decision. Suggest to the counselee that a plan be made to complete each step in a given amount of time. If other people are to be involved, write down their names.

- **Follow-up.** Ask the counselee to check in with you on a certain date to let you know how things are working out for him or her. If the counselee has not arrived at the expected outcome, start the process all over again.

*Adapted from Joan Sturkie and Valerie Gibson, *The Peer Counselor's Pocket Book* (San Jose, Calif.: Resource Publications, 1989), 12, 13.

CROSS-CULTURAL COUNSELING

Suggested minimum time needed for this unit: 4 hours

OPENING

• Read Galatians 3:28. *There is neither Jew nor Greek, slave nor free, male nor female, for you are all one in Christ Jesus.*

• Read 1 Corinthians 9:19–23. *Though I am free and belong to no man, I make myself a slave to everyone, to win as many as possible. To the Jews I became like a Jew, to win the Jews. To those under the law I became like one under the law (though I myself am not under the law), so as to win those under the law. To those not having the law I became like one not having the law (though I am not free from God's law but am under Christ's law), so as to win those not having the law. To the weak I became weak, to win the weak. I have become all things to all men so that by all possible means I might save some. I do all this for the sake of the gospel, that I may share in its blessings.*

• Open with prayer.

• Lead an "I feel" session.

LESSON

GOAL

• To teach basic principles of effective cross-cultural counseling and general characteristics of the major ethnic groups in the United States.

OBJECTIVES

• Trainees will learn the general characteristics of the following five major ethnic groups: white/Caucasian, Asian, African-American, Hispanic, and Native American.

• Trainees will learn basic guidelines for effective cross-cultural counseling.

125

PURPOSE

Explain to the class that skills in cross-cultural counseling (see p. 128) are important for the peer counselor to learn because American society is becoming more culturally diverse and pluralistic. In recent years, we have added a large number of Asians and Hispanics through immigration. The Bible commands us to reach out to all nations and share the Good News of Jesus Christ with them (Matt. 28:19–20). Explain to the class that they will need to know some general characteristics of the major ethnic groups in this country before they can effectively help their peers from such groups. However, the danger of stereotyping and overgeneralizing from such information must be guarded against. Individual differences are also important.

CONTENT

The general characteristics of the five major ethnic groups in the United States (white/Caucasian, Asian, African-American, Hispanic, and Native American) should be briefly reviewed, using the material provided in Chapter Seven.

GROUP PARTICIPATION

EXERCISE 1

If there is a guest speaker who is an expert on cross-cultural counseling speaking at this session, allow time for questions and answers between the speaker and the class. If you present the material from Chapter Seven, there should still be some discussion with the class at the end of the presentation.

EXERCISE 2

Have trainees list feelings, beliefs, habits, attitudes, views, and perspectives that they feel are characteristics of their own cultures. After they have completed their lists and read them to the class, ask the trainees to compare what they have written with what was presented in the class on the five major ethnic groups.

EXERCISE 3

Ask the trainees to think of other Scriptures that support cross-cultural sensitivity and counseling. In addition to the ones already mentioned in this unit (1 Cor. 9:19–23; Gal. 3:28; and Matt. 28:19–20), other passages include John 4:9–10; Acts 4:32; and Acts 8:26–31. You may want to ask the trainees these other questions:

• What do the Scriptures teach about understanding people from other cultures?

• How did Jesus deal with the Samaritan woman in John 4?

• Are there different races or cultures today who do not talk to one another? Who are they? What seems to block their ability to communicate with one another?

• What could we do to improve our relations with people of other cultures?

EXERCISE 4

Instruct the trainees to find a peer from another culture and do a "worldview survey" with him or her (see p. 129).

EXERCISE 5

If there is a trainee in the group from an ethnic or racial minority group, ask him or her to role-play the part of a counselee, while a Caucasian peer role-plays the part of a counselor. This will give the class an opportunity to observe a cross-cultural counseling situation. The problem being role-played should involve cultural issues. For example, if the counselee is Asian, he or she may role-play a conflict between compliance to the curfew time set by his or her Asian parents (say, 10:00 p.m.) and the one set by the parents of his or her Caucasian friends (say, midnight). The role-play could explore how to resolve the conflict.

CLOSURE

• Bring the class back together again as a group and ask if there are any further comments or questions.

• Close in prayer.

You Know You're a Skilled Cross-Cultural Counselor When You . . .

- Share or understand your counselee's worldview.

- Become aware and sensitive to your own cultural baggage and see other cultures as equally valuable as your own culture.

- Are comfortable with differences that exist in terms of race, beliefs, expectations, social backgrounds, and attitudes.

- Understand how ethnic minorities have been treated in the United States, including their oppression because of racism and sexism.

- Understand and use culturally appropriate communication skills.

- Are flexible and sensitive to cultural differences in your use of counseling skills. For example, many ethnic minority counselors prefer an active/directive counseling approach to an inactive/nondirective one.

- Acknowledge your own feelings of anxiety, awkwardness, or even frustration if they are present.

- Are vulnerable and ask your counselee questions about his or her culture that you don't understand.

- Listen and empathize with your counselee.

- Talk to friends from your counselee's culture in order to understand the culture better.

- Read relevant literature both about your counselee's culture and about effective cross-cultural counseling.

- Attend workshops on cross-cultural counseling.

How to Start a "Worldview Survey"

Use these openers to start a conversation with a peer when you want to understand more about his or her culture.

- "Tell me more about your family."

- "Tell me about roles in your family. How do children relate to their parents and grandparents?"

- "What are some important values from your culture regarding education, financial status, and family relationships?"

- "Have you ever experienced prejudice? What happened? How did it affect you?"

- "Will you raise your children differently in relation to culture than your parents have raised you? If so, how?"

STARTING AND ENDING A HELPING RELATIONSHIP

Suggested minimum time needed for this unit: 4 hours

OPENING

- Read Ecclesiastes 3:1. *There is a time for everything, and a season for every activity under heaven.*
- Open with prayer.
- Lead an "I feel" session.

LESSON

GOAL

- To present to the trainees ways of initiating a helping relationship with a teenager and ways of ending it.

OBJECTIVE

- Trainees will learn how to start and how to end a helping relationship.

PURPOSE

- Trainees need to be trained in ways to initiate contact with students.
- Avoiding stereotyping and making hasty judgments also must be addressed.
- Many students may be uneasy about terminating a helping relationship. Knowing when the help has been accomplished or when a referral is needed is an important learning process for the peer counselor.

CONTENT

Counselors will gain counselees in a number of ways. The counselee may be referred by the following:

131

- An adult, such as a Sunday school teacher, parent, or pastor.
- A peer at church or at school.
- The counselee himself or herself.

At the first meeting, the peer counselor introduces himself or herself in a warm, friendly manner, and tells the counselee in what way assistance may be given. The peer counselor will let the counselee know from the beginning that he or she will listen and try to assist, but that he or she will not solve the counselee's problem. The counselee will do that for himself or herself, with some help from the peer counselor. Confidentiality and its limits will be discussed at the first meeting so trust can begin to form and misunderstandings be avoided.

Peer counselors are trained to be nonjudgmental. When a counselee introduces himself or herself, however, a reaction occasionally occurs in the peer counselor. Peer counselors may need to overcome stereotyping ("It is hard for me to be a peer counselor to Jack because he reminds me of a person who has caused great pain in my life previously") or they may find themselves counseling a person who is offensive (body odor, scratching, chewing gum obnoxiously, for instance). Rather than feeling guilty about their feelings toward their counselee, the peer counselor needs to discuss these feelings and ask for suggestions from the class as to how he or she can best handle the situation.

When a peer counselor feels the counselee has successfully solved his or her own problem, the helping relationship should be ended. Sometimes the counselee may want to continue because he or she has become very comfortable talking to the peer counselor and is somewhat hesitant to leave. Continuing the relationship, however, may result in the counselee becoming dependent on the peer counselor.

If the peer counselor has done all that he or she can do, and the counselee still has not solved his or her own problem, then a referral needs to be made (see Unit 10). The peer counselor may refer to a professional or another peer counselor. The leader should stress that the peer counselor need not feel inadequate because the problem has not been solved; rather he or she needs to realize that an important role has been played by acting as a bridge and referring the counselee on to someone else.

GROUP PARTICIPATION

EXERCISE 1

Divide the class into pairs and ask trainees to role-play a situation in which they meet a counselee for the first time.

EXERCISE 2

Divide the class into three groups and give each group a situation where a new counselee presents unique problems (body odor, scratching, chewing gum obnoxiously). Ask the trainees to come up with suggestions as to how to handle the situation.

EXERCISE 3

Divide the class into groups of three and ask a peer counselor and a counselee to role-play a situation where a helping relationship is ending. Ask the third student to be an observer and relay what he or she heard and saw happening. Trainees then alternate roles.

CLOSURE

- Reassure the trainees that they should not feel guilty if they have been unable to help a counselee. Professionals such as psychiatrists and psychologist are not always successful.
- Close in prayer.

REFERRALS AND RESOURCES

Suggested minimum time needed for this unit: 4 hours

OPENING

• Greet everyone at the door as they arrive and ask how they are doing. Give a warm welcome to any guest speakers.
• Read Exodus 18:17–18. *Moses' father-in-law replied, "What you are doing is not good. You and these people who come to you will only wear yourselves out. The work is too heavy for you; you cannot handle it alone."*
• Explain briefly the context of Exodus 18:17–18. Emphasize the need to share the load of peer counseling and to refer to other peer counselors or professional counselors when necessary.
• Open with prayer.
• Lead an "I feel" session.

LESSON

GOAL

• To learn when and how to make referrals and how to use other resources (see the Appendix).

OBJECTIVE

• Trainees will become aware of peer counseling situations that may require referrals to professional counselors, other peer counselors, or other resources. They will learn how to make a referral (see p. 138).

PURPOSE

The class needs to know that there are times when a counselee should be referred to someone else (see p. 138). The peer counselor should not feel inadequate when the situation is beyond his or her capabilities. An important task has already been performed by the peer counselor through helping the counselee identify the problem and see the need to contact another person. When a peer counselor has accomplished this, he or she then acts as a bridge to professional help. The counselee should know that the peer counselor is still available after the professional help has been completed.

CONTENT

A peer counselor should refer a counselee when he or she lacks the skills (or experience or knowledge or emotional stamina or time) to begin or continue counseling.

Peer counselors need to be familiar with agencies and persons in the community to whom they may refer their counselees. See Exercise 4 (on p. 137) and use it as a way for your peer counseling trainees to work as a group to assemble a list of local, regional, and national referrals that includes psychiatrists; psychologists; marriage, family, and child counselors; suicide prevention centers; physicians; pastors; Alcoholics Anonymous chapters; child abuse agencies; and the department of social services.

GROUP PARTICIPATION

EXERCISE 1

Ask the class to look over the list of possible referrals in the Appendix. Lead a discussion in which you review the agencies that tend to be used more frequently in the context of a peer counseling ministry. Emphasize the strong points of the various resources.

EXERCISE 2

Ask for a volunteer from the class to role-play the part of a counselee, with you, the leader, role-playing the part of the peer counselor. Assume that the counselee is severely depressed. He or she will be in immediate need of a referral to a mental health professional (a licensed psychologist or psychiatrist, for example). As the leader, you role-play appropriate and supportive responses to the counselee, suggesting a referral to a professional counselor. Make statements like the following:

> It must be very painful and difficult for you to feel so down all of the time. I believe that you need and deserve more expert help than I can give. I would like to suggest that you see a Christian professional counselor who can provide the kind of help that you will benefit from. I have the name and telephone number of such a person. How do you feel about seeing this counselor?

EXERCISE 3

Divide the class into groups of three. Ask one person to role-play the part of a counselee needing a referral and one to play the peer counselor. The third person observes the role-play and provides feedback.

EXERCISE 4

Ask pairs of trainees to select one name from a list of local referral agencies (in your city or county). The trainees then call that agency and report back to the class with the following information: name of agency, address, telephone number, hours the office is open, ages accepted, cost (inquire if there is a sliding scale), and the name of a contact person. The trainees will make a master list of these local resources and keep it for future reference.

CLOSURE

- Ask if there are any further questions or comments.
- Close in prayer.

Outside Help Should Be Sought When the Counselee . . .

- Demonstrates aggressive behavior
- Abuses drugs or alcohol
- Talks about suicide or doing bodily harm to another person
- Needs medical help
- Is being physically, mentally, or sexually abused
- Seems to be emotionally unstable
- Requests professional help
- Needs legal assistance

How to Refer*

1. Learn what resources are available in your community so the most appropriate place or person may be contacted.

2. Check with the community resources before referring, so you will know that an opening is available for your counselee.

3. Let your counselee know why you feel he or she should be referred, while at the same time give as much support as possible.

4. Explain to your counselee the reason for each of the referral options you've shared with him or her.

5. Involve the counselee as much as possible in the decision to refer. If the counselee "claims ownership" for the decision, he or she will probably be more faithful keeping scheduled appointments.

6. Encourage the counselee to make his or her own appointment, for you may not have the information needed to schedule such an appointment.

7. Help the counselee plan how he or she will get to the appointment and decide if another person is needed to go along.

8. Show your continuing care for the counselee even after he or she has been referred, and be ready to support the counselee during and after the time he or she is seeing a professional.

*Adapted from Joan Sturkie and Valerie Gibson, *The Peer Counselor's Pocket Book* (San Jose, Calif.: Resource Publications, 1989), 32-33.

GRADUATION AND BEYOND

After the peer counselors have completed their basic training, they look forward to their graduation ceremony—usually an evening event preceded by a potluck dinner. Here are the typical parts.

GRADUATION EVENING

Banquet

Let the peer counselors be in charge of the banquet—mailing invitations, decorating the room, deciding who will bring what food, planning the program, cleaning up. The young people will enjoy doing all of these things and will claim more ownership of the event. You'll need to make sure everything is going as scheduled, but don't jump in and take charge, no matter how tempting it may be. Even in this celebration, you want to empower your young people. If you insist on taking the power back once the classes are over, you'll never accomplish your goal. Besides, you have enough to do already—so save your energy!

Wonderful things happen at these banquets. Dale, for example, was so shy he hardly said a word when he first entered the peer counseling class. It took him several weeks before he volunteered any comments in the "I feel" session other than, "I pass." Gradually Dale began to trust and gain confidence. When it came time to role-play, he hesitated at first, but then seemed to feel at ease when assuming a role. Dale's public speaking abilities blossomed in class, but I must admit I was still surprised when he asked if he could serve as master of ceremonies at the banquet.

I had no need to worry. The night of the banquet, Dale was an eloquent speaker as he told the audience how just a few months previously he had been afraid to speak even before his own classmates, and how being in peer counseling had given him the confidence to get up now before several hundred parents and peers. Several years after his graduation, Dale mentioned to me how important that banquet night had been for him.

Presentation of Peer Counseling Shirts

Several weeks before the banquet, the peer counselor trainees may want to select, order, and pay for peer counseling shirts. These are usually sweatshirts, and the trainees select the color and the words to be printed on the shirt. The words may say simply "Peer Counseling" or "Peers Helping Peers" or "Listening with Love." Some may also include a Scripture reference, such as John 13:34. The night of the banquet, these shirts are presented to the peer counselors, along with a graduation certificate.

It is important to stress that no one but a trained peer counselor may wear these shirts (siblings who are accustomed to borrowing clothes may not know the messages the shirt's wearer imparts). Anyone wearing the shirt is, in effect, saying, "I am here for you. I am trained to listen and help you with your problems." The peer counselors wear these shirts with pride. They have earned them through weeks of preparation.

Presentation of Certificates

Some youth leaders design special certificates for their present and future groups. These are particularly nice because the name of the church or parachurch organization, the level of training (beginning or advanced), and the purpose of the certificate will already be on it. This will leave only the trainee's name, date of the event, and signature of the program leader (youth director and/or pastor) to be added. Or you can get generic certificates from a stationery store and add in all the information.

These certificates convey the message that the peer counselors have completed a course of training on peer counseling—they are *not* licenses for the peer counselors to do professional counseling or to claim special competence in particular counseling methods.

Commissioning Service

The church or parachurch organization should commission the peer counselors. This is a particularly meaningful part of the evening because the commitment of the church or parachurch organization to these teenagers is demonstrated. The young people, in turn, dedicate themselves to Christian service by serving as a peer counselor.

Ask the pastor of the church or president of the parachurch organization to conduct this part of the program. If these people cannot be present, then someone representing them should certainly be in attendance.

The purposes of the commissioning are as follows:

• Recognition of peer counseling as a Christian ministry.
• Validation of the training for the counselor.
• Identification of the counselor with the sponsoring organization.
• Collective ownership of those attending the commissioning and by the constituency of the organization.[1]

After the commissioning, a time of dedicatory prayer may serve as the benediction for the evening.

Schedule the elements of graduation to fit your group. You can present shirts and certificates during the banquet, saving the commissioning for a regular church service. Or do the entire ceremony during a church service if a banquet is impossible. Mix and match the elements with different settings in whatever way fits your trainees and your church or organization.

Recognition of Advanced Training

At the banquet also recognize peer counselors who have completed advanced training (see below). Certificates signifying completion of advanced peer counseling training will be presented.

Encourage active peer counselors to attend the banquet, even if they are not being honored for completing advanced training. They still need to show their support for the beginning trainee graduates and their fellow peer counselors.

ADVANCED PEER COUNSELOR TRAINING

Advanced peer counseling training is not covered in this book, yet it is an essential component of a comprehensive peer counseling training program. Conduct it after the basic training program is completed. *Advanced Peer Counseling*, scheduled for publication in the fall of 1993, will cover such issues as crisis counseling, peer pressure, school-related issues, family issues, child abuse, drugs and alcohol, sexuality, pregnancy, AIDS, eating disorders, codependency, death and loss, suicide, war, spiritual issues, cults, and the occult. It can be used as an advanced training course manual for Christian peer counselors.

Training definitely should continue, ideally on a weekly basis. Several benefits are gained by these advanced training sessions:
• The group continues to have contact with each other. It is important for the group to continue to bond. Young people feel a continuing sense of belonging and acceptance. Christian fellowship is an important by-product of these meetings.
• Teenagers have the opportunity to discuss any problems they may be having in counseling their peers. By meeting at least once a week, the peer counselors will gain valuable input and validation from the supervisor and the peer counselors.
• The skills the peer counselors learned in the beginning class are strengthened. This may be accomplished by continued use of exercises, such as role-playing.
• You can introduce some new material on topics such as crisis counseling, sexuality issues, and eating disorders—and learning continues.

BEYOND TRAINING

After peer counselors are trained, they are equipped with

skills for life. It is not that important whether they continue to function as designated peer counselors in the future, because they have learned communication skills. They are now better prepared to listen and send effective messages to a husband or wife, an employer or employee, a friend or neighbor. They can understand and withhold judgment of people who are different from themselves. They are readily able to reach out to a neighbor.

The young people who continue to serve their church or organization as peer counselors will have unlimited opportunities open to them for Christian service. They may want to do only one-on-one counseling, or they may want to lead support groups for their peers. Their desire may be to reach into the community where their impact on non-Christians will be more greatly felt. Serving as a peer counselor and listening to the hearts of the lonely in convalescent hospitals, senior citizen homes, protective centers for children, or jails may be the mission of some young people.

The future impact of some of these teenage peer counselors will be documented in schools, hospitals, churches, halfway houses, and private offices as they go to college and prepare to become professional counselors. Because of their experience as a peer counselor, some of these young people decide that this is the type of work they want to do in their adult life. Their spiritual gifts—encouragement or exhortation, wisdom, mercy, hospitality—are discovered, and they feel God has made known his will for their lives. They will be doing Christian service (many in a secular world) for years to come, and they will be training a new generation of peer counselors to do the same things they did as teenagers.

FULL CIRCLE: A CASE STUDY

A few months ago I received a call from a young woman who is completing her master's program in counseling. Elaine was a trainee in the first peer counseling class I taught on a high school campus, and I have watched her progress ever since.

Now she is ready to become a professional counselor herself.

Elaine called in a reflective mood. She had just returned home from another day on a high school campus as an intern. The internship was a part of her final course before graduation. "I am going to apply for a job as a high school counselor," she told me, "and I am going to start a peer counseling program as soon as possible." She paused a moment. "I can't tell you how important that peer counseling class was to me. For the first time I felt like I was listened to, accepted—that my opinions were important. Who I was really mattered to the other people in that class. We all cared so much for each other." Another pause. "I just want to make it possible for other kids today to experience what I experienced, to feel the love I felt."

This sort of love, experienced on a public high school campus, can and should be felt among our young people in Christian youth groups. There are peers who need to be trained so another circle will be completed: a Christian youth worker trains a peer counselor who becomes a Christian youth worker who trains other peer counselors.

What a marvelous circle to complete.

LIST OF RESOURCES AND REFERRALS

ADOPTION

Concerned United Birthparents (CUB). (515) 262-9120. Support for birthparents in coping with adoption.

Yesterday's Children. (312) 545-6900. Self-help for persons who have been separated from their biological families through foster care, adoption, death of parents, or divorce.

AIDS

National Association of People with AIDS. (202) 429-2856. Network of people with AIDS.

ALCOHOLISM

Alcoholics Anonymous. (212) 686-1100. Members share experiences and support one another.

Al-Anon Family Group. (212) 302-7240. Support and help for family members of alcoholics.

Alateen/Ala-Preteen/Alatot. (212) 302-7240. Help (coping skills) for children who live with an alcoholic.

Adult Children of Alcoholics. (213) 464-4423. Help for adults who were raised in an alcoholic, dysfunctional environment.

Students Against Driving Drunk (SADD). (617) 481-3568. Alerts students to dangers of drinking and driving.

ALZHEIMER'S DISEASE

The Alzheimer's Disease and Related Disorders Association. (312) 853-3060. Assistance for caregivers of Alzheimer's patients.

ANOREXIA/BULIMIA

Anorexia Nervosa and Associated Disorders, Inc. (312) 831-3438. Provides information on self-help groups, therapy, and referrals to professionals.

American Anorexia and Bulimia Association. (201) 836-1800. Provides support for anorexics, bulimics, and their families.

CHILD ABUSE

Parents Anonymous. (800) 421-0353. Help for parents who are abusing their children.

Incest Survivors Anonymous. (213) 428-5599. Help for incest victims.

Incest Survivors Resource Network. (516) 935-3031. Educational resources on all aspects of incest.

C. Henry Kempe National Center for the Prevention and Treatment of Child Abuse and Neglect. (303) 321-3963. Treatment, education, national resource library, legal services for child abuse.

DEATH

Compassionate Friends. (312) 990-0010. Support and understanding to parents and siblings grieving a child's death.

Survivors. (619) 727-5682. Help for those experiencing grief after the death of a loved one.

DELINQUENCY

Youth Guidance (Youth for Christ, USA). (312) 668-6605. The largest Christian ministry to young people in trouble. Has some residential care programs.

DISABILITY

National Association of the Physically Handicapped. (614) 852-1663. Promotes public awareness of the needs of the disabled.

Siblings for Significant Change. (212) 420-0776. Trains siblings of handicapped persons to be advocates for themselves and their families.

Catholics United for Spiritual Action (CUSA). (201) 437-0412. A correspondence organization for the handicapped and chronically ill. Open to persons of all faiths. Emphasis on spiritual values and mutual support.

DIVORCE

Committee for Mother and Child Rights. (914) 238-8672. Information and support pertaining to custody problems related to divorce.

Grandparents' Children's Rights, Inc. (517) 339-8663. Information for grandparents who are denied visitation rights with grandchildren.

DEPRESSION AND MENTAL ILLNESS

National Association for Mental Health. (703) 528-6408. Information and referrals for mental health problems.

American Association of Psychiatric Services for Children. (202) 371-1033. Help for children with psychiatric needs.

National Depressive and Manic Depressive Association. (312) 939-2442. Support and information for manic depressives, depressives, and their families.

Youth Emotions Anonymous. (612) 647-9712. Program for young people (ages thirteen to nineteen) to help develop healthy emotions, attitudes, and habits, using a twelve-step program.

National Sibling Network. (612) 872-1565. Support and information for siblings of persons with mental illness.

DRUG ABUSE

Cocaine Anonymous. (213) 559-5833. Fellowship of men and women who share their experiences and help each other recover from addiction.

Narcotics Anonymous. (818) 780-3951. Recovering addicts meet regularly to help each other stay clean.

National Drug Abuse Center. (202) 654-3582. Information pertaining to all aspects of drug abuse.

Drugs Anonymous. (312) 874-0700. Self-help, twelve-step program based on A.A. for those who want to recover from chemical addiction.

Families Anonymous. (818) 989-7841. Fellowship of relatives and friends of people involved in drug abuse.

Just Say No Foundation. (800) 258-2766. Helps communities form "Just Say No Clubs" for groups of children (ages seven to fourteen) who are committed to not using drugs.

FAMILY

Stepfamily Association of America, Inc. (301) 823-7570. Information and advocacy for stepfamilies.

International Youth Council. (301) 588-9354. Teens from single-parent homes get together to share ideas and problems and plan fun activities.

GAMBLING

Gamblers Anonymous. (213) 386-8789. Fellowship of men and women who share experiences with each other to recover from compulsive gambling.

Gam-Anon Family Groups/Gam-A-Teen Groups. (718) 352-1671. Provides help for family members and friends of compulsive gamblers.

HOMOSEXUALITY

Homosexuals Anonymous. (215) 376-1146. A Christian fellowship of men and women who have chosen to help each other live free from homosexuality.

Presbyterians for Lesbians/Gay Concerns. (201) 932-7501. Support for lesbians and gays in the Presbyterian Church. Advocates a ministry with homosexuals. Uses peer counseling.

LEGAL ASSISTANCE

American Bar Association. (202) 331-2200. Information and referral service.

Christian Legal Society. (703) 560-7314. Networking ministry of Christian lawyers, professors, and students. Information and referral service.

OVERWEIGHT

Overeaters Anonymous. (213) 320-7941. A fellowship of people who meet to help one another understand and overcome compulsive overeating. Uses a twelve-step program.

T.O.P.S. (Take Off Pounds Sensibly). (414) 482-4620. Fellowship of friends and relatives of compulsive overeaters.

PREGNANCY

Department of Health and Human Services/Office of Adolescent Pregnancy Programs. (202) 472-5588. Government-sponsored information and referrals pertaining to youth pregnancy programs.

National Pregnancy Hotline. (800) 356-5761. Help pertaining to pregnancy and alternatives to abortion.

RUNAWAYS

National Runaway Switchboard. (800) 621-4000. Will provide free long-distance calls home for runaways. Confidentiality respected. Counseling and referrals.

Operation Peace of Mind. (800) 231-6946. Will relay information to parents from kids "on the run" without revealing location.

SMOKING

American Lung Association. (212) 245-8000. Information and referral service for smokers.

California Smokers Anonymous. (213) 474-1161. Assists smokers to become free from smoking obsession by using a twelve-step program.

SUICIDE

Students Against Suicide. (714) 361-9401. Organization especially for teenagers. Formed to open up communication between teens and parents through play production. Information and referrals.

Survivors of Suicide (SOS). (414) 442-4638. Help for families and friends of suicide victims.

TOLL-FREE NATIONAL HELPLINES

Adoption	(800) To-Adopt
AIDS	(800) 243-2437
Alcohol	(800) Alcohol
Anorexia/bulimia	(800) Bash-STL
Attorney referral	(800) 624-8846
Blindness	(800) 424-8666
Cancer	(800) 4-Cancer
Child abuse	(800) 422-4453
Cocaine	(800) Cocaine
Diabetes	(800) 223-1138
Disabilities	(800) 54-Health
Domestic violence	(800) 333-Safe
Drug abuse	(800) 662-Help
Dyslexia	(800) ABCD-123
Education	(800) 638-9675
Hospice	(800) 331-1620
Marijuana	(800) 677-7433
Missing children	(800) 843-5678
Pregnancy	(800) 356-5761
Runaways	(800) 621-4000
Venereal disease	(800) 227-8922
Youth (drug problems, runaways, homeless)	(800) 999-9999

Introduction

1. Siang-Yang Tan, *Lay Counseling: Equipping Christians for a Helping Ministry* (Grand Rapids: Zondervan, 1991), 61–81; Joan Sturkie, *Listening with Love: True Stories from Peer Counseling*, 2d ed. (San Jose, Calif.: Resource Publications, 1987), 210.

Chapter One—Why Peer Counseling?

1. Centers for Disease Control, cited in *Youthworker Update* 6, no. 3 (November 1991): 3.
2. *Wall Street Journal*, cited in *Youthworker Update* 6, no. 4 (December 1991): 3.
3. Centers for Disease Control, cited in "The Unhealthy Facts of Life," *Newsweek Special Issue: The New Teens* (Summer/Fall 1991): 57.
4. Eugene Strull, M.D., "Alarming Incidence of Illness among Teenagers," *Los Angeles Times* (April 18, 1987), Part 2, 2.
5. Centers for Disease Control, cited in *Youthworker Update* 6, no. 3 (November 1991): 3.
6. Centers for Disease Control, cited in *Youthworker Update* 6, no. 4 (December 1991): 4–5.
7. *Statistical Abstract of the United States 1990*, 11th ed. (Washington, D.C.: U.S. Department of Commerce, Bureau of the Census, 1990), 177.
8. Strull, "Alarming Incidence of Illness among Teenagers," 2.
9. Carnegie Council on Adolescent Development, *Turning Points: Preparing American Youth for the 21st Century* (New York: Carnegie Council on Adolescent Development, Carnegie Foundation, 1989).
10. National Assessment of Educational Progress (NAEP), cited in *Turning Points*.
11. Vincent D'Andrea and Peter Salovey, *Peer Counseling Skills and Perspectives* (Palo Alto, Calif.: Science and Behavior Books, 1983), 3.

Chapter Two—The Bible and Peer Counseling

1. Siang-Yang Tan, *Lay Counseling: Equipping Christians for a Helping Ministry* (Grand Rapids: Zondervan, 1991), Chapter 3.
2. Tan, *Lay Counseling*, Chapter 3.
3. An excellent resource for biblical teaching, as well as insight and research about specific psychological problems, is *Christian Counseling: A Comprehensive Guide*, Rev. ed. (Waco, Tex.: Word, 1988), by Gary Collins. It covers a wide range of revelant topics, from anxiety to counseling the counselor.

Chapter Five—Selecting Your Peer Counselor Trainees

1. Siang-Yang Tan, *Lay Counseling: Equipping Christians for a Helping Ministry* (Grand Rapids: Zondervan, 1991), 100, 102.

Chapter Seven—Cultural Diversity in Peer Counseling

1. David J. Hesselgrave, *Counseling Cross-Culturally* (Grand Rapids: Baker, 1984), 20.

2. Norman D. Sundberg, "Research and Research Hypotheses about Effectiveness in Intercultural Counseling," as cited by Hesselgrave in *Counseling Cross-Culturally*, 146–47.
3. Gary Collins, *Innovative Approaches to Counseling* (Waco, Tex.: Word, 1986), 148.
4. Collins, *Innovative Approaches to Counseling*, 149.
5. For summaries of the Asian, African-American, Hispanic, and Native American cultures, the authors are indebted to Derald W. Sue, *Counseling the Culturally Different* (New York: John Wiley, 1981), 113–255. See also, Derald W. Sue and David Sue, *Counseling the Culturally Different*, 2d ed. (New York: John Wiley, 1990).
6. Sue, *Counseling the Culturally Different*, 52.
7. Sue, *Counseling the Culturally Different*, 61.
8. See Collins, *Innovative Approaches to Counseling*, 155–57; and Sue, *Counseling the Culturally Different*, 105–07.
9. Sue, *Counseling the Culturally Different*, 105.
10. David W. Augsburger, *Pastoral Counseling across Cultures* (Philadelphia: Westminster, 1986), 21.

TRAINING COURSE

Unit 3—Developing Active Listening Skills

1. Norman Wakefield, "Learn to Be a Listener," *Counsellor's Journal*, CWR4 (1981): 10.

Unit 5—Developing Self-Awareness and Building Self-Esteem

1. Kenneth Blanchard, *The One Minute Manager* (New York: Morrow, 1982), 19.
2. David Seamands, *Healing Grace* (Wheaton, Ill.: Victor, 1988).
3. California Department of Education, *Toward a State of Esteem: The Final Report of the California Task Force to Promote Self-Esteem and Personal and Social Responsibility* (Sacramento, Calif.: Bureau of Publications, California Dept. of Education, 1990).

Conclusion: Graduation and Beyond

1. Joan Sturkie and Gordon Bear, *Christian Peer Counseling: Love in Action* (Waco, Tex.: Word, 1989), 45.

Augsburger, David W. *Pastoral Counseling across Cultures.* Philadelphia: Westminster, 1986.

Backus, William, and Marie Chapian. *Telling Yourself the Truth.* Minneapolis: Bethany House, 1980.

Baldwin, Carol L. *Friendship Counseling: Biblical Foundations for Helping Others.* Grand Rapids: Zondervan, 1988.

Beattie, Melody. *Codependent No More.* San Francisco: Harper and Row, 1987.

Benson, Dennis C., and Bill Wolfe. *The Basic Encyclopedia for Youth Ministry.* Loveland, Colo.: Group Books, 1981.

Burns, Ridge, with Noel Becchetti. *The Complete Student Missions Handbook.* Grand Rapids: Youth Specialties/Zondervan, 1990.

Christian Broadcasting Network. *The Christian Counselor's Handbook.* Wheaton, Ill.: Tyndale House, 1987.

Collins, Gary R. *Give Me a Break: The How-to-Handle-Pressure Book for Teenagers.* Old Tappan, N.J.: Revell, 1982.

—————. *Innovative Approaches to Counseling.* Waco, Tex.: Word, 1986.

—————. *Christian Counseling: A Comprehensive Guide.* Rev. ed. Waco, Tex.: Word Publishing, 1988.

Crabb, Lawrence J., Jr. *Effective Biblical Counseling.* Grand Rapids: Zondervan, 1977.

—————. *Inside Out.* Colorado Springs: NavPress, 1988.

—————. *Understanding People: Deep Longings for Relationship.* Grand Rapids: Zondervan, 1987.

D'Andrea, Vincent, and Peter Salovey. *Peer Counseling Skills and Perspectives.* Palo Alto, Calif.: Science and Behavior Books, 1983.

Dobson, James. *Love Must Be Tough: New Hope for Families in Crisis.* Waco, Tex.: Word, 1983.

——————. *Preparing for Adolescence.* Ventura, Calif.: Regal, 1978.

Foster, Richard. *Celebration of Discipline: The Path to Spiritual Growth.* Rev. ed. New York: Harper and Row, 1988.

Glenn, H. Stephen, and Jane Nelsen. *Raising Children for Success.* Fair Oaks, Calif.: Sunrise Press, 1987.

Hesselgrave, David J. *Counseling Cross-Culturally.* Grand Rapids: Baker, 1984.

Kesler, Jay, ed. *Parents and Teenagers.* Wheaton, Ill.: Victor, 1984.

Kubler-Ross, Elisabeth. *On Death and Dying.* New York: Macmillan, 1969.

Lindquist, Stanley E. *Action Helping Skills: Manual for Peer Counseling.* Fresno, Calif.: Link Care Press, 1976.

Lynn, David, and Mike Yaconelli. *Teaching the Truth about Sex.* Grand Rapids: Youth Specialties/Zondervan, 1990.

Madara, Edward J., and Abigail Meese. *The Self-Help Sourcebook.* 2d ed. Nutley, N.J.: Hoffmann-LaRoche, Inc., 1988.

Martin, Grant L. *Counseling for Family Violence and Abuse.* Resources for Christian Counseling, Vol. 6. Waco, Tex.: Word, 1987.

McCoy, Kathleen. *Coping with Teenage Depression: A Parent's Guide.* New York: New American Library, 1982.

McDowell, Josh. *What I Wish My Parents Knew about My Sexuality.* San Bernardino, Calif.: Here's Life Publishers, 1987.

Miller, Paul M. *Peer Counseling in the Church.* Scottsdale, Pa.: Herald Press, 1978.

Moore, Joseph. *A Teen's Guide to Ministry.* Liguori, Mo.: Liguori Publications, 1988.

Myrick, Robert D., and Tom Ervey. *Youth Helping Youth.* Minneapolis: Educational Media Corporation, 1985.

Myrick, Robert D., and Don L. Sorenson. *Peer Helping: A Practical Guide.* Minneapolis: Educational Media Corporation, 1988.

Olson, G. Keith. *Counseling Teenagers: The Complete Christian Guide to Understanding and Helping Adolescents.* Loveland, Colo.: Group Books, 1984.

──────────. *Why Teenagers Act the Way They Do.* Loveland, Colo.: Group Books, 1987.

Painter, Carol. *Friends Helping Friends: A Manual for Peer Counselors.* Minneapolis: Educational Media Corporation, 1989.

──────────. *Leading a Friends Helping Friends Peer Program.* Minneapolis: Educational Media Corporation, 1989.

Peck, M. L. *Youth Suicide.* New York: Springer Publishers, 1985.

Penner, Clifford, and Joyce Penner. *A Gift for All Ages: A Family Handbook on Sexuality.* Waco, Tex.: Word, 1985.

Phillips, Maggie. *The Peer Counseling Training Course.* Revised and expanded by Joan Sturkie. San Jose, Calif.: Resource Publications, 1991.

Posterski, Donald. *Friendship: A Window on Ministry to Youth.* Scarborough, Ont.: Project Teen Canada, 1986.

Rice, Wayne. *Junior High Ministry.* Rev. ed. Grand Rapids: Youth Specialties/Zondervan, 1990.

Richards, Lawrence O. *The Believer's Guidebook.* Grand Rapids: Zondervan, 1983.

Sturkie, Joan. *Enjoy Your Kids: Enjoy Your Work.* Waco, Tex.: Word, 1991.

──────────. *Listening with Love: True Stories from Peer Counseling.* San Jose, Calif.: Resource Publications, 1987.

Sturkie, Joan, and Valerie Gibson. *The Peer Counselor's Pocket Book*. San Jose, Calif.: Resource Publications, 1989.

Sturkie, Joan, and Gordon Bear. *Christian Peer Counseling: Love in Action*. Waco, Tex.: Word, 1989.

Sturkie, Joan, and Marsh Cassidy. *Acting It Out*. San Jose: Calif.: Resource Publications, 1990.

Sue, Derald W. *Counseling the Culturally Different*. New York: John Wiley, 1981. See also: Derald W. Sue and David Sue. *Counseling the Culturally Different*. 2d ed. New York: John Wiley, 1990.

Swihart, Judson J., and Gerald C. Richardson. *Counseling in Times of Crisis*. Waco, Tex.: Word, 1987.

Tan, Siang-Yang. *Lay Counseling: Equipping Christians for a Helping Ministry*. Grand Rapids: Zondervan, 1991.

Van Cleave, Stephen, Walter Byrd, and Kathy Revell. *Counseling for Substance Abuse and Addiction*. Waco, Tex.: Word, 1987.

Van Pelt, Rich. *Intensive Care: Helping Teenagers in Crisis*. Grand Rapids: Youth Specialties/Zondervan, 1988.

Varenhorst, Barbara, with Lee Sparks. *Training Teenagers for Peer Ministry*. Loveland, Colo.: Group Books, 1988.

Wallerstein, J. S., and J. B. Kelly. *Surviving the Breakup: How Children and Parents Cope with Divorce*. New York: Basic Books, 1980.

Ward, Waylon O. *The Bible in Counseling*. Chicago: Moody Press, 1977.

Worthington, E. L., Jr. *Counseling for Unplanned Pregnancy and Infertility*. Waco, Tex.: Word, 1987.

—————. *How to Help the Hurting: When Friends Face Problems with Self-Esteem, Self-Control, Fear, Depression, Loneliness*. Downers Grove, Ill.: InterVarsity Press, 1985.

—————. *When Someone Asks for Help: A Practical Guide for Counseling*. Downers Grove, Ill.: InterVarsity Press, 1982.

Wright, Norman. *Crisis Counseling*. San Bernardino, Calif.: Here's Life Publishers, 1985.

—————. *How to Have a Creative Crisis*. Waco, Tex.: Word, 1987.

—————. *Training Christians to Counsel*. Eugene, Ore.: Harvest House, 1977.

Yaconelli, Mike, and Jim Burns. *High School Ministry*. Grand Rapids: Youth Specialties/Zondervan, 1986.

INDEX TO FORMS AND REPRODUCIBLE PAGES

ALPHABETICAL LISTING